Education for Citizen Action

CHALLENGE FOR SECONDARY CURRICULUM

Fred M. Newmann

University of Wisconsin, Madison

McCutchan Publishing Corporation
2526 Grove Street
Berkeley, California 94704

ISBN: 0-8211-1305-4
Library of Congress Catalog Card Number: 74-30963

© 1975 by McCutchan Publishing Corporation
All rights reserved

Printed in the United States of America

FOR MY MOTHER AND FATHER

Preface

Education should help students engage in intelligent action. In spite of considerable rhetoric on this topic, the relationship between action and education has not been closely examined in statements of educational aims, in designs for curriculum, in the daily experience of students, or in teacher education programs. This book builds in some detail a conception of education for competent action in one area of human concern—public affairs. It is deliberately written for a variety of readers: social studies educators; university students and faculty in curriculum, philosophy of education, and teacher education; secondary school curriculum coordinators, administrators, counselors, and teachers in diverse subjects; and, more generally, anyone interested in helping public education take a more vigorous part in improving the system of consent of the governed in the United States. Persons with interests in alternative schools, experiential education, student volunteer programs, or the general topic of community involvement will also find relevant material.

Our purpose here is to offer a systematic rationale for exerting influence in public affairs as a central priority in secondary schools, to outline a general conception of student competencies implied by this goal, and to anticipate issues in the program and environment of secondary schools that must be faced if the proposed curriculum were to be implemented. We do not provide details of an actual curriculum, successful teaching strategies, or evaluation devices. Nor can we offer a staff development program to assist in implementation. Each of these matters must be subjects for future development, which this book is intended to generate.

Though I am the sole author, the editorial "we" is used to communicate my feeling for the book as the outcome of collective effort that required assistance from many sources. This is not to attribute individuals and institutions acknowledged below any responsibility for what appears, but to recognize the considerable help I received from them.

Funding from the United States Office of Education, TTT (Training of Teacher Trainers Program, grant no. OEG-0-70-2054-721), under the leadership of Donald Bigelow, provided resources for high school students, teachers, graduate students, and university staff in Madison to participate in citizen action projects as part of secondary school and Ph.D. programs from 1969-1973. While directing this program, I gained valuable insights about education for citizen action.

High school students, their parents, and teachers and administrators in the Madison public schools offered their support and participation in the Community Issues Program, a citizen action course at James Madison Memorial High School, 1969-1971. This course, described in Chapter 4, became a major experiential base for many of our concepts and recommendations. Conan Edwards, Richard Gorton, and Clinton Barter provided administrative support. Michael Brockmeyer, Bruce Gregg, George Shands, Steve Sheets, and Calvin Stone offered creative teaching, perceptive analysis, and a warm welcome to the university contingent. A similar program, with less direct university involvement, was initiated at Park High School in Racine, thanks to the cooperation of Donald Thompson and James Eastman of the Racine Public Schools. Former Ph.D. students and TTT staff at the University of Wisconsin worked in these and other efforts to help high school students take action on issues in their community. I learned much from working with the following individuals in this capacity: Kenneth Addison, Robert Alexander, Kenneth Dowtin, George Gates, James Leming, David Marsh, Eugene Parks, W. Eugene Robertson, Stephen Timmel, and Conrad Worrill.

The publications board of the National Council for the Social Studies encouraged me to write a manuscript for social studies teachers on social action in the curriculum. This manuscript was originally intended for the NCSS, but technicalities in their publishing policy prevented publication by the NCSS. Nevertheless, I remain grateful to NCSS reviewers—Robert Burek, Gary Manson, and Anna Ochoa—for their helpful comments.

Preface

A grant from the Graduate School at the University of Wisconsin provided research leave for the summer of 1974, offering a timely opportunity to consolidate previous work.

A number of colleagues in Madison and elsewhere reacted to part or all of the manuscript in various stages of preparation. Their criticism and suggestions are deeply appreciated: Tom Bertocci, Dan Conrad, Jack Dennis, David Harris, Diane Hedin, Herbert Kliebard, Barry Lefkowitz, Jean McGrew, Howard Mehlinger, Richard Merelman, Ralph Mosher, John Palmer, David Purpel, Francis Schrag, Michael Scriven, Charles Slater, Norman Sprinthall, Stanley Wronski.

Several people were instrumental in the publishing process: David Purpel, the editor who wanted to publish it; John McCutchan, the publisher; Peter Krug who organized the Appendix; Genny Mittnacht, a cheerful, expert typist; Pat Burhans, a reliable, all-around secretary; and Rita Howe, a talented copy editor.

Finally, a special note of thanks is reserved for a few people, close to me, who generously offer feedback, not only on the formal manuscript but also on spontaneous ideas that occur in our daily work together. I have relied much on the intelligence of Joy Newmann, Michael Apple, Alan Lockwood, and Gary Wehlage.

Fred M. Newmann
Madison, Wisconsin
November 1974

Contents

PREFACE		v
INTRODUCTION		1
CHAPTER 1	Environmental Competence as an Educational Goal	12
CHAPTER 2	Exerting Influence in Public Affairs	41
CHAPTER 3	An Agenda for Curriculum Development	76
CHAPTER 4	Program Structure	109
CHAPTER 5	Choices in Teaching	138
CONCLUSION		161
APPENDIX	A. Organizations Supporting Community Involvement Curriculum	169
	B. Directory of Illustrative Community Involvement Programs	171
	C. Illustrative Citizen Action Organizations	183
REFERENCES		187
INDEX		195

Introduction

Sources of Powerlessness

Discussion on topics as diverse as Watergate, the environmental crisis, school desegregation, or the youth culture repeatedly raises the dismal prospect that most of us have little control over our destinies. Despite familiar rhetoric about ideals of self-determination and consent of the governed being the keystones of democracy, there is a suspicion, among youth and adults, that these rights do not, and perhaps never did, exist in America, and there is a growing sense of powerlessness, alienation, and pessimism about the future. The lack of hope that one might, in a meaningful sense, control one's existence, and the tendency to face daily demands of school, work, or family with passive resignation rather than assertive vitality can be explained in several ways.

Whether one assumes conscious conspiratorial action by elite classes or the victimization of everyone by the system, there are those who insist that this society's political-economic structure requires that the majority of people be exploited and kept in a passive role so that a powerful elite can rule. A variety of forces—private property, profit and competition, modern technology that centralizes power in vast bureaucratic hierarchies, meritocracy and credentialing, or a "natural" human tendency to dominate one's fellows—are held responsible, and, for those who hold this general view, fundamental change in the underlying structure of the political-economic system is the only way to increase citizens' control over their lives.

Another explanation that is consistent with, but does not logically follow from, the first concentrates on specific attitudes and discriminatory practices that place insurmountable obstacles in the path of oppressed groups. Youth cannot govern their affairs because mistrusting adults pass laws to ensure their isolation. Overt and covert manifestations of racism deny people of color the right to control their lives, and sexism is equally powerful in denying self-determination for women. Other groups, such as the mentally retarded, the physically handicapped, the elderly, the poor, homosexuals, unwed mothers, those with criminal records, or Vietnam veterans, are also deprived of equal social participation through discriminatory attitudes and practices. If one holds this view, the liberation of oppressed groups requires changes in specific laws to guarantee equal treatment. There must also be an attitudinal change: more acceptance of human diversity, with special empathy for those who suffer owing to forces beyond their control.

A third explanation for this sense of powerlessness is perhaps the most pessimistic, for it suggests that the problems we face are inherently so complex that man will never solve them through deliberate, rational intervention. Population growth and escalating consumption levels threaten human survival. Cultures with vastly divergent values, now in positions of economic interdependence, insist on maintaining political independence. Corporate bureaucratic empires created by "developed" countries are beyond the comprehension of their own leadership. The multitude of variables involved in understanding the short- and long-term effects that an apparently simple event such as a change in the price of oil has on constituencies around the world confounds almost any prediction about the consequences of our actions. Those who support this view argue that to try to change the system or specific practices within it might result in an illusion of control, but it would be self-deceptive. Ultimately, they believe that rational human intervention is a myth; we must accept the inability to control our destiny as a condition of existence.

Each orientation is true to some extent, but none by itself is sufficient to explain the inability of large numbers of persons to exert deliberate influence upon public policy. Even if all economic, political, and social barriers to citizen participation were abolished and if public issues were less complex, many people would still be incapable of effective participation because of personal incompetence. A wide-

Introduction

spread lack of knowledge, skills, and attitudes conducive to the exercise of influence accounts, at least in part, for the alleged failure of the democratic ideal. It would make sense, therefore, to increase individual competence as a first step in exerting influence in public affairs.

If skills in policy research, persuasion, and organization were increased significantly in the citizenry at large, this would at least eliminate personal incompetence as a factor contributing to powerlessness. If this variable could be removed, other explanations could be more easily tested. To the extent that alternative theories of powerlessness are legitimately contested, we ought to provide options for each person to act in accord with his own conclusions. Note, for example, that, to pursue the remedies implied either by the first theory (system change) or the second (policy reform), a person needs the ability to make an impact in definite directions. If competence in the general exercise of influence were increased, each citizen would have more choice in deciding whether to change the system, change specific policies, or drop out (the third theory). It is from this perspective that this book defines and justifies a conception of citizen competence to exert influence in public affairs and proposes an agenda for curriculum development to meet that end.

Pitfalls of Citizenship Education

For decades educators and laymen have proclaimed a concern for citizenship education. Since one justification for state-supported compulsory education is the preservation of the democratic state, there is wide agreement that public schools should teach children how to participate in a democracy as responsible citizens. Yet youth in the 1950's distinguished themselves by apathy; many of those in the 1960's, by hyperactivism. In the United States the quality of citizen participation always seems to fall somewhat short of an ill-defined ideal. We criticize ourselves for being apathetic and uninvolved, unwatchful and unconcerned enough to allow abuse of power and crime at all levels of government. At the other extreme, there are activists who express passionate concern on selected issues but are accused of acting impulsively or of making irrational judgments based on incomplete information. We seem to be either too loyal and trusting of public authority or too cynical and uncommitted to participate. The apparent failure to properly educate citizens for active participation in democracy is by no means the sole responsibility of schools. Here as in other areas schools have been expected to undertake more than they alone can reasonably accomplish. It is evident, nevertheless, that public schooling has not done as much as it could to educate for effective citizen participation.

The notion of citizen participation has been defined in such a way that educational practice neglects the most crucial component in democratic theory: the right of each citizen to *exert influence in* (in contrast to "thinking critically about" or "taking an active interest in") public affairs. The curriculum may emphasize the duty of everyone to keep informed, to register, to vote, and even to contact one's representatives between elections. The study of social issues may assist students in deciding which policies to favor or oppose. Yet instruction of this sort does not realistically deal with what it takes to make an impact on public policy. Little or no attention is paid to action research or to developing skills in persuasion and organization. A person who wants to exert influence finds little help in current approaches to citizen education.

Rather than aiming directly at the exercise of influence, citizenship education has been preoccupied with:

Academic disciplines. This approach assumes that, if students gain knowledge in history, the social sciences, and other disciplines as they are organized and disseminated through university-based scholarship, they will be better equipped to make intelligent judgments in civic matters.

Legal-political structure of government. Courses in civics, American government, law, and other areas try to inform students about formal aspects of the legal-political system (how a bill becomes a law, checks and balances in government, systems of representation, constitutional rights). It is assumed that such knowledge is required for effective citizen participation.

Social problems. Students gain information on such public issues as war, crime, discrimination, poverty, pollution, and drugs. Some courses may even seek to persuade students to support specific public policies (disarmament, consumer protection). It is assumed that knowledge of issues will improve citizen participation.

Critical thinking and inquiry. The emphasis here is on the intellectual process of reaching conclusions, rather than the acquisition of substantive knowledge. Topics such as logical inference, validation of empirical claims, recognition of assumptions and biases, inconsistency in argument, propaganda techniques, and the use and misuse of statistics are studied to cultivate students' critical abilities, which, it is assumed, will help them protect their rights and pursue their interests as citizens.

Democratic values. This approach, often integrated with themes above, concentrates on teaching students to favor as legitimate values such concepts as democracy, majority rule, minority rights, due process of law, equality, citizen participation, and consent of the governed. The development of positive attitudes toward these principles is presumed to be the basis of a vigilant and active citizenry.

While each of these themes is potentially relevant to the exercise of influence, actual curricula in their behalf have not concentrated on the problems of a citizen struggling to make an impact. Knowledge from the academic disciplines is rarely applied to the civic dilemma of choosing when to take a stand and how to do it effectively. Instruction on legal-political structure usually ignores informal channels of influence (money, social affiliations, political debts, bureaucratic empires) and the dynamics of power at levels of government close to the student's life (Who has the power to determine the budget for the school play?).[1] While instruction on social problems seems directly helpful to students' exercise of influence, it usually avoids the study of what students might do to affect the destiny of the problems examined. Likewise critical thinking skills are seldom applied to personal choices about ways to exert influence. Instead, inquiry and critical thinking is most often directed to questions arising from the academic disciplines (What was the most important cause of the Civil War?). Finally, the teaching and preaching of democratic values often seem hypocritical to students. Unqualified endorsement of values fails to recognize the existence of genuine conflicts among the "sacred" principles themselves. The school is not run democratically, and the curriculum fails to help students reconcile the gap between the ideals promulgated and the realities of the world around them.

---

1. An exception is the Comparing Political Experiences Program currently being developed through the Social Studies Development Center, Indiana University. A major thrust of this curriculum is to teach high school students to study their school as a political system. Gillespie and Patrick (1974) provide a conceptual framework for the program.

Considered as a whole, these dimensions of citizenship education are plagued by an orientation that, in subtle ways, tends to communicate unworkable notions of citizen participation. The underlying orientation tends to emphasize the importance of students learning to understand, describe, or explain reality, rather than exerting an impact upon it; reflection at a general, abstract level, rather than at the specific and concrete level of analysis; issues of national or international scope to the exclusion of problems faced directly by more local constituencies such as school, voluntary association, or neighborhood; forms of citizen participation that are either highly visible and militant (strikes and demonstrations) or relatively impotent (a letter to your congressman), and neglect persistent, behind-the-scenes activities of effective citizens.

A more adequate orientation would recognize the significance of helping students to affect their environment, not simply to comprehend its effects upon them; of recognizing concrete issues on which positions must be taken without interminable abstract analysis; of acting upon local issues (Should the school be required to use recycled paper?), in contrast to distant national issues (What should Congress do to preserve natural resources?); and of adopting "invisible," perhaps unglamorous styles of action appropriate for typical citizens (How can one convince the principal to sponsor a special symposium on women's rights?), in contrast to dramatic approaches used by "superstar" activists who might organize a march on Washington or a national boycott. Because the proposed agenda for curriculum (Chapter 3) emerges from a highly focused, interdisciplinary analysis of the knowledge, skills, and attitudes required for humans to exert influence in public affairs, perhaps it can avoid the weaknesses in prevailing approaches to citizenship education.

Varieties of Community Involvement and Social Action

To remedy some of the problems noted, many advocate programs of "community involvement," "action learning," "volunteer work," "youth participation," or "social action" for high school students. These phrases strike responsive chords for educational critics and reformers. "Community" bespeaks a desire to build a sense of collective interdependence, to break down walls that isolate individual students from each other, and to end the isolation of formal instruction

Introduction

from life in the world at large. It conveys a sense of unity, relatedness, a holistic vision as an antidote to the fragmentation, specialization, and individual competition that make it difficult for humans in this society to relate to each other on a "human" level. "Involvement" suggests that education ought to help students become engaged and excited through personal investment in the intrinsic value of learning, rather than forcing them to play the game of school, apathetically going through the motions in a detached, alienated manner. "Action" represents assertiveness as opposed to passivity, a tendency to exert influence on reality, to take some responsibility for rather than be controlled by events, a propensity for "doing" rather than only thinking or talking.

The phrases carry symbolic power for those who seek to make education more "relevant" to the needs of students and their society, but we must not adopt them too quickly as panaceas for the ills of education. Educators who work toward a more "relevant" curriculum may feel a sense of community in their mutual struggle to change curriculum, but even those who claim to be working toward community involvement, youth participation, and social action may not seek common goals. Slogans can obscure distinct and sometimes contradictory philosophies or objectives of education.

At the outset, then, we should identify different interpretations of and objectives for community involvement and social action. Educators have cited the following activities to illustrate how secondary students engage in community involvement or social action.

1. Door-to-door canvassing for a political candidate.
2. Tutoring elementary students.
3. Visiting a home for the elderly.
4. Conducting an attitude study on racial prejudice.
5. Organizing a cleanup of city parks.
6. Internships with adults in business, government, the professions.
7. Inviting adults from the community to speak at school.
8. Making a film about a local social problem.
9. Working to abolish a school dress code.
10. Marching in a peace demonstration.
11. Seeking more parent and student control of school policy.
12. Studying the history of local institutions.
13. Participating in a sensitivity group.

Are these actually examples of community involvement, social action, both, or neither? If we define community involvement as any activity in which students work in or with groups, almost all items on the list would qualify. If we restrict the definition to any activity in which students work outside the school with adults who are not professional educators, items 2, 4, 7, 9, and 13 would not seem to qualify. Even this restricted conception of community involvement, however, embraces activities as diverse as visiting a home for the elderly, marching in a peace demonstration, and studying the history of local institutions. If social action is defined as any activity in which students demonstrate concern for a social problem, it would be difficult to disqualify any item on the list, for each in some way could reflect a concern for some social issue. Under this broad definition, "concern" might be demonstrated by conducting a study, participating in volunteer work, or active advocacy, either in or outside of school. A narrower definition might restrict social action to any activity in which students actually attempt to influence public policy in the community beyond the school, in which case perhaps only items 1 and 10 would qualify.

Educators often quarrel over whether a given program truly represents a certain approach. Is your curriculum *really* an example of "inquiry," "human relations," "interdisciplinary studies," or "student-centered learning"? As illustrated, some disagreements on these matters can be resolved by more precise definitions of key terms. Often, however, definitional disagreements have their origins in disputes over the objectives of education. For this reason we must be alert to the possibility that escalating semantic controversy about the value of activities may belie unmentioned distinctions among objectives.

Rather than press immediately for precise definitions, let us first differentiate among activities on the above list by recognizing the difference between an educational activity and an educational objective.[2] Then we can note the variety of objectives that any given activ-

---

2. In deemphasizing definitions here, we do not wish to avoid the issue. Community involvement activities could be defined as those in which students participate, primarily outside their school with adults who are not professional educators, and with youth who need not be peers in their school. We can define social action as an activity in which a student attempts to exert influence on public policy. Thus, most social action efforts would be a type of community involvement, but community involvement would also include activities with many other purposes.

Introduction

ity might serve. In visiting a home for the elderly, for example, teacher and students might have as their objective any of the following:

A. Providing a community service by giving companionship to senior citizens.
B. Conducting a study of elderly people as a vehicle to learning in the disciplines of psychology, sociology, or history.
C. Exploring student interest in a particular career choice—professional care of the elderly.
D. Gathering information to be used in a social campaign to persuade public officials to allocate more financial resources to care for the elderly.
E. Improving students' abilities to communicate with persons different from themselves.
F. Having a learning experience in the "real" world, that is, outside of the school where learning tends to be excessively verbal and abstract.

Some of these objectives may complement each other (A and C), but others may not (B and D). Thus, before passing judgment on the educational value of an activity it can be helpful to articulate which objectives it is intended to serve. If multiple objectives seem possible, priorities must be established and compatibility determined.

Having made the distinction between activities and objectives, it should be clear that community involvement activities can serve a whole range of objectives.

1. For the academician the activities could be pedagogical devices for illustrating theory, findings, insights that have been contributed by a number of disciplines in the humanities, or the physical or social sciences. For the inquiry teacher community involvement could assist in the formation of hypotheses, the collection and analysis of data (for example, students making observations about human behavior or probing public and private records).

2. The vocational educator might see community involvement and social action as orientation for careers and vocations through internships with practicing social workers, journalists, programmers, lawyers, mechanics, politicians, and police.

3. The humanitarian or good Samaritan may see such activity as providing manpower for needed public services (environmental cleanup, day care, consumer education, tutoring) that are not currently provided by private and public institutions.

4. The experiential educator could favor such activities as a means

of ensuring that learning is rooted in the "reality" of the learner rather than in the often abstract, formal, excessively verbal nature of conventional curriculum.

5. For a political conservative, community involvement and social action might be a means of demonstrating the basic legitimacy of existing political institutions. As students become deeply involved in social problems, perhaps they will learn that existing institutions operate as fairly and as efficiently as can reasonably be expected and that lack of solutions is due more to the complexity of the problems than the nature of the political system. Through direct participation in decision-making processes, students may well learn that the existing structure, though not perfect, is the lesser of evils. By involving students with persons in government, business, and the professions who have this orientation and can point to apparent progress in several areas, the view might be persuasively communicated.

6. For the political revolutionary, community involvement and social action could serve to expose basic contradictions and injustice in the system, demonstrating the need for radical restructuring of institutions. Involving students with certain groups (racial minorities, the poor) who have suffered and been exploited and whose grievances have not been redressed by legitimate "channels" would strengthen this view.

7. For the advocate of group awareness and group development, community involvement and social action could signify a desire to break down the isolation and alienation of persons from themselves and from each other, thus enabling a more "human" or "caring" community to develop. One example would be the formation of intimate groups of students who work together on a project of their choice, in or out of school.

8. To place students in roles that require caring for others and taking responsibility for one's actions in the "real world" beyond school may interest the developmental psychologist as a vehicle to promote growth in cognitive complexity, moral reasoning, or the accumulation of ego-strength.

9. An advocate of community control or the use of paraprofessionals in schools might want to increase local input, to use local resources to improve the teaching of the conventional curriculum.

If objectives as diverse as these were all included in a school's community involvement and social action program, the program could

Introduction

conceivably support activities in or outside of school; it might involve few or many adults; it could include conventional didactic as well as unstructured experiential learning; students could be relatively unsupervised or strictly supervised by professional educators; students might be involved in various combinations of study and research, volunteer service, apprenticeships, or political advocacy—working in groups or individually. The tremendous diversity of objectives could generate a plethora of activities that would confuse students, teachers, and adults in the community.

Because community involvement and social action activities can be offered in pursuit of such diverse and potentially conflicting educational objectives, such activities should not be endorsed unconditionally. Educators should specify the objectives sought and then determine whether particular forms of community involvement and social action might assist in their achievement. I have argued previously for the importance of community- and action-oriented education, and this note of caution does not dampen that commitment. For a general movement in this direction to be educationally effective, however, we need a more comprehensive educational rationale, a more specific statement of objectives, and a more systematic model for curriculum than we now have. Beginning with a general rationale for helping students exert impact in their environment, this book attacks each of these problems.

CHAPTER 1

Environmental Competence as an Educational Goal

Environmental Competence

There are fundamental differences among educational philosophies; yet virtually all imply some notion of competence. How much emphasis schools should give to different types of competence is debatable, but that schools ought to assist in the development of student competence must be taken as given. Competence is defined as the ability to behave in such a way, or to use one's efforts in such a manner, as to produce the consequences that one intends.[1] Competence is reflected, therefore, in purposeful behavior, not in activity that might be considered involuntary, aimless, or mindless.[2] For example, person A intends to replace a flat tire with a spare, consciously trying to behave in a way that will achieve that result. If successful, we conclude that the person had the "competence" to change a tire. Person B joins a group with the intention of learning to say to others what he or she really feels. If, at the end of the group sessions, the person senses that "true" messages are getting across and if group members confirm this (perhaps by informing the speaker what messages were being received), some skills in communication must have been gained. Person C may wish to comprehend a physics unit on electricity well enough to earn an A grade on an examina-

---

1. This is consistent with the work of White (1959) and Smith (1968), but it is not identical to the definitions given by either.
2. The free will-determinism debate can blur the distinction between purposeful and voluntary versus aimless and involuntary behavior. Yet material in Hampshire (1959), White (1968), and Brand (1970) adds up to an adequate philosophical case for this distinction.

Environmental Competence as Educational Goal 13

tion. If the examination accurately measures comprehension of that material and the person earns the A grade, we could conclude that person C had developed some competence in the subject of electricity.[3]

Failure to achieve intended consequences of one's actions, however, should not necessarily be attributed to a lack of competence in the person who harbors the intentions. Person A could conceivably fail, not for lack of technical skill, but because the spare tire had been stolen. Person B might have more difficulty in expressing feelings at the end of the group sessions because of the group leader's deficiencies. Person C may fail the examination because of distressing family problems that interfered with concentration. The point here is not to ascribe fault or responsibility when people are unsuccessful, but rather to suggest that to educate is, to a large extent, to help persons attain the consequences they intend. This goal may be summarized as teaching for competence.

This psychologically based definition, where the key to competence is a congruence between personal intentions and outcomes, might be questioned. First, it can be argued that many student intentions should not be supported through public education. Some desires may be considered immoral (learning to cheat, steal, or exploit others); others, too personal or private (learning to make love or communicate with God); others, trivial (learning to wash dishes or to use the telephone book). Admittedly, this definition is broad enough to recognize the "competence" of a thief, a lover, or a dishwasher, but it does not imply that such forms of competence must be nurtured by schools. The definition of competence as the ability to act in accord with intentions does not prevent educators from deciding which kinds of intentions and consequences ought to be cultivated in schools or from choosing to influence students to hold some kinds of intentions in preference to others.

These are matters for further deliberation. For example, a child may wish to solve mathematical problems and succeed in solving the

---

3. The examples of competence given here raise the question of whether ability to act in accordance with one's intentions is a general trait (e.g., comparable to what has been measured by tests of verbal or quantitative aptitude), or whether it must be broken down into an almost infinite number of specific tasks. Brand (1970) offers clarification on difficulties in assessing the presence or absence of "abilities" of various sorts. Chapter 5 discusses issues in evaluating ability to exert influence in public affairs.

problem 2 + 2 = _____ . The fact that the student behaved in accord with intentions on that problem is an indication only of competence in solving that single problem. If one is led to believe that, in having solved this problem, one has become a competent mathematician capable of solving other sorts of problems such as quadratic equations, the student will have an erroneous view of competence in mathematics. There are, of course, high standards of achievement that may exceed student intentions. These standards need to be communicated to students so that they can decide whether they intend to achieve levels of competence consistent with such standards. In teaching for competence, educators have an obligation to help students critically evaluate their own intentions and to acquaint them with forms of competence and standards of excellence of which they may be unaware. In this sense the goals or intended consequences entertained by students should be studied with care, not unconditionally endorsed, a point that will be explained in more detail later.

Valuable learning occurs serendipitously, not simply through the rational pursuit of activities designed to bring about the learner's consciously intended consequences. A student may put great effort into the study of mathematics, not because he or she can identify any particular desired consequences, but because it is intrinsically satisfying. Another may join the orchestra primarily to be with friends or to please parents. The first student may eventually become a mathematician and the second a professional musician, but neither outcome was consciously planned. In many instructional situations, teachers' notions of competence are probably hidden from, or meaningless to, the students, and yet students still learn. The fact that persons develop competence "accidentally" or through processes in which they do not consciously aim toward ultimate performance goals is an observation on the process of learning that need not modify our definition. It is useful, however, as a means of informing the teacher that, while the student may have no intention of becoming an "intelligent consumer," he or she does enjoy playing a consumer role in exchanging play money with peers. The teacher who intends to develop mathematical competence may employ students' intentions in peer play as a pedagogical device in teaching mathematical or consumer competence. In such cases the teacher makes a prediction that, in the long run, the student will desire the ability to act so as to avoid being exploited as a consumer. That type of competence can conceivably be taught to persons who, at the time of instruction, may not share that explicit goal. Instruction for competence is, however, easier to accomplish when the goals of both teacher and student are identical.

Given a definition of competence as the ability to behave in ways that bring about the consequences one intends, we can inquire about different types of intentions and consequences that could presumably occupy the attention of those deciding on curriculum. Many of the consequences we intend involve making an impact in the environment beyond oneself: repairing an automobile, giving comfort to a troubled friend, electing the candidate of our choice, or producing a film. Each goal represents an attempt to influence, change, or affect phenomena (objects, people, events) external to oneself, and the test of one's competence lies largely in the extent to which the influence exerted in the environment was consistent with one's intentions.

In contrast, self-oriented intentions are less concerned with making an impact in the external environment and more concerned with affecting one's mind, sensitivities, or body. In learning to read, to analyze a poem, to understand the causes of war, or to comprehend algebraic proofs, a central goal is often to interpret or make sense of various phenomena, that is, to develop one's mind to the point where order or meaning can be experienced. Cognitive manipulation of symbols in such activities is not necessarily undertaken to make an impact on the phenomena. Other kinds of self-oriented intentions include attempts to "get in touch" with one's true feelings, to develop in oneself new forms of personal awareness, to clarify one's values as to what one "really" wants in a course, a job, or a mate. The desire to keep oneself in good health, or to exert control over one's body, represents another type of goal aimed inward toward self rather than outward toward control or manipulation of the external environment.

Intentions cannot often be neatly classified as being oriented primarily toward impact on self or on external environment; nor can they be easily inferred from participation in a given activity. A student may work arduously during an election campaign to put a new person in office (an environment-oriented goal), but claim that one of her main reasons for participating was to learn something about politics (a self-oriented goal). Another might put great effort into studying economics texts, trying apparently to comprehend rather than to exert influence in the economic system. Perhaps, however, the person's long-term goal is to alter the federal tax structure. The period of rigorous "self-oriented" study is seen mainly as preparation for making an impact in the external environment. The existence of a variety of human motives, including possible differences between immediate and long-range goals, can make it difficult to determine the salience of intentions oriented primarily toward making an impact on self or on reality external to self.

We can observe, however, that some activities, regardless of intention, involve the participant more directly than others in attempts to influence the environment (people, objects, and events external to oneself). An individual who, in the process of organizing a day-care center, runs meetings, writes promotional literature, gives speeches, and solicits funds, engages in more direct and complicated manipulation of the environment than the person who reads a history book. Playing a piano concerto involves a more complicated exercise in controlling the environment than simply listening to music. The distinction here is not between self versus environment, but between activities requiring a high versus a low degree of manipulation of phenomena external to oneself. As with the classification of intentions or goals, the classification of activities cannot eliminate all ambiguity. There are, nevertheless, reasonably clear examples to illustrate the distinctions. In Table 1, the goals are accompanied by corresponding activities that might be undertaken in their pursuit. The table further illustrates an independence between goals and activities: that both self- and environment-oriented goals may be pursued through activities requiring both high and low degrees of environmental manipulation and control.

These distinctions do not comprise an exhaustive scheme for classifying human goals and activities. They are meant to lay the groundwork for recognition of a particularly important dimension of human competence, that is, the ability to act in accord with the intentions one has for making an impact in the environment external to oneself. For lack of a better term, this is called *environmental competence*. It should not be equated with the ability to practice conservation or to forestall ecological disaster. Although such objectives could be included as examples, the scope is broader, embracing the diverse and multitudinous ways in which people wish to exert influence in the world. A major point of this book is to call attention to the fact that

TABLE 1
Examples of goals oriented toward environment and self and of activities requiring high and low degrees of environmental manipulation-control

Goals	Activities grouped according to degree of environmental manipulation-control required	
	High	Low
Major impact on environment		
a. Start counseling center for runaways	a. Arrange a meeting with school administrators and police	a. Read studies on the problem
b. Teach a young child to read	b. Convince a discouraged child to keep trying	b. Check out books from library
c. Rebuild a car	c. Tune the engine	c. Change a tire
Major impact on self		
d. Clarify personal values	d. Organize group discussion in which people will be honest with you	d. Think about values
e. Understand chemistry	e. Operate lab equipment	e. Read chemistry books
f. Keep physically fit	f. Get rebounds and make baskets in competition	f. Run

much of the competence toward which we aspire requires exerting impact in the environment beyond oneself. Formal education, however, has concentrated on goals oriented more exclusively inward, toward self.

The emphasis on environmental competence is not intended to neglect the significance of human intentions oriented toward self, such as the desire to experience pleasure by reading about, listening to, observing, or reflecting upon, rather than manipulating, events in the external environment. "Self-oriented" goals also give direction to the pursuit of competence in general.[4] In a sense the quest for any sort of personal competence, including the ability to make an impact in the external environment, represents a concern for self-develop-

---

4. Our definition of competence in general as congruence between intentions and outcomes is broader than White's (1959), for while White views competence exclusively as producing intended effects in the environment, ours includes the ability to produce intended effects upon oneself. Our "environmental competence" is thus equivalent to White's "competence."

ment, which might cast doubt on the power of the distinction. Analogous distinctions could be developed, perhaps, through such concepts as external versus internal, public versus private, or active versus passive forms of competence. These problems cannot be satisfactorily resolved here, but the concept of environmental competence is still useful in leading us to inquire about the extent to which education does and should help people exert influence upon people, objects, and events beyond themselves.

The concept can be further developed by constructing a taxonomy that identifies different types of environmental competence. For example:
A. Physical—ability to have an impact on objects
   1. Aesthetic (painting a picture)
   2. Functional (building a house)
B. Interpersonal—ability to have impact on persons
   1. Nurturing relationships (caring for a baby or friend)
   2. Economic relationships (selling a car)
C. Civic—ability to have an impact in public affairs
   1. Public electoral process (helping a candidate win election)
   2. Within interest groups (change policy priorities of a consumer protection group).

These categories are incomplete. They overlap and represent different levels of abstraction; they also indicate the need for refinement of the notion of environmental competence as a first step in applying the concept to curriculum development. An expanded taxonomy of environmental competence would give educators a comprehensive set of alternatives from which to choose, and we need a debate over the relative emphasis that ought to be given to different ways of affecting one's environment. This book develops in some detail that aspect of environmental competence involving the exercise of influence in public affairs, but leaves to future efforts the generation of curricula for other types of environmental competence.[5]

Environmental Competence, Action and Reflection

There may be a tendency to equate "environmental competence" with "action," and to separate both from "reflection." According to

---

5. The Panel on Youth (1974) presents a notion of socialization that implies, but does not spell out, a variety of environmental competencies that go beyond the exercise of influence in public affairs. See also Coleman (1972a).

Environmental Competence as Educational Goal

some basic definitions, this would be inappropriate. Environmental competence is a proposed educational goal, defined as the ability to engage in behavior that leads to one's intended consequences in the environment. Action is defined as purposeful behavior in which a person attempts to exert influence in the environment.[6] Clearly, much behavior cannot be classified as action, for it is nonpurposeful. Examples include behavior considered aimless, unconscious, nondeliberative, reflexive, or involuntary. There is also a considerable range of purposeful behavior—reading a novel, meditation, rock climbing—that does not involve making an impact on the environment. "Action" is reserved for behavior accompanied by a conscious intent to bring about some effect in the environment.[7]

We can participate in arduous and frenetic action, trying in various ways to have an impact in the world, but involvement in action alone is no indication of environmental competence. A person's actions could be singularly unsuccessful in fulfilling intended consequences, or they might be gloriously successful, but neither conclusion could be drawn from knowing only that one had "acted." Moreover, involvement in action is no guarantee that one is learning environmental competence. Some action might be counterproductive to the development of environmental competence, as when one persistently attempts impossible projects and then, because of continuous failure, refuses to act at all. Finally, some persons might have great ability to affect the environment, but choose not to do so, illustrating possession of environmental competence without action. Chapter 2 establishes that action is a necessary, though not a sufficient, experience in the learning of environmental competence. The point is made here simply to show that they should not be equated. Instead, action is one means toward the goal of environmental competence. The educational aim is not action alone, but the ability to engage in "successful" action (that which yields outcomes consistent with one's intent).

Action is often distinguished from reflection and, in spite of Dewey's considerable efforts, the erroneous dichotomy of "thinking" versus "doing" persists. According to our definition, action presupposes reflection, for in order to act one must have conscious

---

6. This is consistent with philosophical analyses of action provided by White (1968) and Brand (1970).
7. If behavior can be construed as observable motions or moves, then action consists of behavior plus the conscious thought, purposes, or intentions employed to guide behavior.

thoughts as to one's aims. Though the quality of reflection may vary, it is impossible to act without reflecting about one's intent. Since environmental competence is the ability to undertake "successful" action, it also presupposes reflection, probably of a more sophisticated nature than is required for action alone. It will become clear by the end of Chapter 3 that, in proposing a curriculum for environmental competence in public affairs, we propose a large dose of reflection. It is possible, of course, to reflect but not to act, and this characterizes most curricula in schools and colleges where learning is oriented toward developing descriptions and explanations of various phenomena, or even fantasy or creative thought, but where one's cerebral energy is not directed at exerting an impact upon the world. Because schools have so consistently isolated reflection from attempts to affect reality beyond oneself, thinking itself has unfortunately been interpreted as being different from action ("thinking" versus "doing"). As proposed here, however, reflection can logically, that is, through definition, be integrated with action and environmental competence.

Do Schools Teach Environmental Competence?

To what extent does the school curriculum honor environmental competence as an educational objective? It is difficult to make quantitative empirical claims about actual effects of schooling on student competence, for adequate research on this topic does not exist.[8] We can, however, observe the relative emphasis given to environmental competence in subjects studied, approaches to instruction, criteria for evaluation of student achievement, and the general social milieu of schools. Such observations will be analytic, generally descriptive, and it is assumed that the reader has had sufficient experience with schools to assess their accuracy.

In general, schools tend to ignore, and in some cases clearly oppose, the development of environmental competence. This does not seem to be the result of conspiracy or of conscious, deliberate efforts

---

8. Prevailing measures of achievement do not assess environmental competence, but rather the student's ability to comprehend, decode, and symbolize materials presented in school. The extent to which schooling itself actually affects performance on even these measures, however, is a matter of hot dispute (Jencks *et al.*, 1972; Mosteller and Moynihan, 1972).

by those who control schools. On the contrary, many educators would probably agree that an ultimate purpose of education is precisely to help people function in their environment. In spite of such rhetoric, however, the nature of schooling usually exhibits a paucity of direct emphasis on environmental competence.

First, consider substance or content in the secondary curriculum. In studying English, mathematics, science, social studies, the arts, or vocations, do students ever inquire how man has affected the world, can affect it, or should affect it? In a sense, almost all subjects lend themselves to such questions, but the potential is rarely realized. Students in history may be taught general causes of important events (the American Revolution, the Civil War, the desegregation decision of 1954). They do not, however, study the struggles of individuals laboring to affect the outcomes of those events. In English curricula devoted to the study of literature or communication skills, students might examine the nature of interpersonal relationships, but seldom do they focus on specific competencies needed to affect another person in the way that was intended. Mathematics and science teachers may point out monumental effects on the environment of applying their disciplines, but students are not taught to use such subjects to increase their ability to affect their own environments. There are important exceptions, some of which are noted below, but the critical mass of content in school curricula lacks topical emphasis on individual and collective efforts to affect one's environment.

The process of instruction, regardless of subject area, usually places students in the passive role of receiving knowledge. For much of their school life they are supposed to absorb material by attending to presentations of teachers; by using textbooks and other media; by answering, orally and in writing, questions posed by teacher or text; and by observing other classmates' responses to these questions. In short, the student must usually assume an unassertive, inactive, almost docile role, allowing the environment to impinge upon oneself, rather than taking initiative to influence it. To be sure, there exists within schools great potential for a more active learning process. In laboratories, shops, studios, libraries, and instructional materials centers many students already participate in activities requiring significant degrees of environmental control. If such facilities are used to support independent study and if independent study occupies a central part of the curriculum, many students can function more autonomously and manipulate their own learning environments. But a subtle and overwhelming message can find its way through even these processes: that the purpose of instruction is to help the student understand the world, rather than to affect it.

Approaches to student evaluation may be the best indicators of the goals a school values. A school that valued environmental competence would probably offer tests, observation schemes, interviews, or other ways of gathering evidence on the extent to which students produced the effects they intended on objects, people, events, and so forth. This evaluation would need to differentiate among diverse types of action and to determine when apparent student failure was due primarily to incompetence that might be remedied through instruction or to other variables over which neither teacher nor learner has meaningful control. To my knowledge, no evaluation scheme of this sort has been developed. Criteria for evaluating student achievement still stress mastery of content or skills (reading, mathematics, writing, research techniques) needed to gain more self-oriented knowledge. The student receives virtually no feedback on the extent to which he or she can make an impact in the world.

A number of practices, considered departures from conventional schooling, might be cited as evidence for curriculum movement in the direction of education for action: fewer restrictions on student conduct; increased student choice in selecting courses and topics within courses; increased emphasis on inquiry skills, critical thinking, and analysis of values; increased attention to social issues; increased use of community resources; and increased stress on career education. While each of these reforms is potentially consistent with the goal of environmental competence, none logically requires, or is often applied to, its pursuit. There are reasons why each of them, considered in turn, should not necessarily be viewed as equivalent to education for environmental competence.

Fewer restrictions on student conduct. Relaxation of dress codes, increased freedom of movement during school hours, and greater freedom of political expression may expand opportunities for students to take responsibility for, and play a more active role in, determining their own destiny. Yet these "extracurricular" rights or freedoms are not usually integrated into instruction itself, and the curriculum pays slight attention to the problem of using such freedoms intelligently. Decreasing restrictions on student conduct may generate more autonomous behavior on the part of students, but, to the extent that such behavior is mindless, impulsive, or aimless, environmental competence will not be nurtured.[9]

Increased student choice in selecting courses and topics within courses. Opportunity for independent study in combination with a smorgasbord of diverse electives could conceivably enhance environmental competence. Unfortunately, however, most of the alternative courses and topics also ask the student to describe or explain the world as it is or was, rather than to develop a plan for making some impact on it. Questions that educators pose to students as "alternative topics" often only distantly relate to a student's desire to affect reality.

Increased emphasis on inquiry skills, critical thinking, and analysis of values. Many schools attempt to move beyond mere transmission of information and toward the cultivation of skills in deductive and inductive logic, observation and analysis of empirical data and "original source materials," and critical examination of the structure of argument and debate. Some offer instruction on the evaluation and justification of prescriptive, normative, or value claims. The development of cognitive process in these areas is crucial if students are to deliberate rationally about probable consequences of alternative choices, and much of the curriculum proposed in Chapter 3 relies upon these processes. Too often, however, the application of these skills does not focus on matters germane to the students' exercise of influence. Instead, central questions tend to arise from the framework of an academic subject. In a history course, for example, students ask, "What evidence is available on Abraham Lincoln's motivation for going to war to 'save the union'?" They may complete thorough and sophisticated research on such a problem, gaining skills that may be transferred to questions more directly related to their own action. Yet, we must recognize the probable irrelevance of this kind of problem to their own choices about exerting influence in the world. On those few occasions when students are asked to defend their own actions, the available choices are hypothetical and not to

---

9. The Center for New Schools (1972) found that, in alternative schools, the exercise of expressive freedom was not accompanied by positive student action to affect the destiny of the learning community over which students could, if they wished, exert a large measure of control.

be acted upon as part of school instruction: "What would you do if you were Lincoln?"

Increased attention to social issues. Numerous materials dealing with social issues now used in many courses could conceivably help students study the exercise of influence in political, economic, and social contexts. They may study origins and causes of poverty, the nature of racial discrimination, the extent of pollution, and recent court rulings on civil liberties, but unless instruction devotes significant attention to citizens' efforts to exert influence on such problems, social issues can become as unrelated to development of environmental competence as the study of topics more obviously oriented inward (for example, learning the structure of symphonic composition). A three-year curriculum in analysis of public controversy (Oliver and Newmann, 1967-1973; Newmann and Oliver, 1970; Oliver and Shaver, 1974) taught analytic skills in taking a stand on public issues, but devoted little attention to how students could implement beliefs that they had so "rationally" developed. Exposure to social issues, whether through formal instruction or the media, can even convey the message that most public policies are too complicated, too unmanageable, or too easily influenced by "evil" forces. If this were the dominant lesson in the study of social issues, one's sense of efficacy would understandably decrease.

Increased use of community resources. Many have urged that schools become better integrated with the community-at-large. One way of achieving this has been for adults with a variety of experiences to come into the schools and for students to venture out into the community. Student volunteer programs, guest speakers, field trips, student internships, teacher aides and paraprofessionals in schools, work-study programs, student research projects, and surveys on community life can all be seen as efforts in this direction. Many of them should be applauded for their potential to increase environmental competence. It must be recognized, however, that some uses of community resources give students more information about how the environment affects them than how they might affect it. The noted Citizenship Education Project (1955) intended to further the cause of active citizen participation in many colleges and universities. Almost all of its efforts were spent on studies of community issues, however, and not on helping students act to affect the outcomes of the issues. The Appendix provides examples of community-oriented

Environmental Competence as Educational Goal

projects undertaken recently by adolescents around the country, some of which are more directly oriented toward environmental competence than others.

Increased stress on career education. The recent concern for career education, which emphasizes the importance of a productive life at work, might be seen as helping students exert more control over their destiny. Conclusions on this matter would depend upon the nature of instruction in particular situations, but there are at least two dangers in such an interpretation. To the extent that curriculum conveys the notion that one must "fit in" to existing or predicted career options, it fails to teach a student that one might create a career role for oneself, perhaps by influencing an institution to change certain career models to accommodate personal interests. (This problem is especially salient for persons seeking meaningful part-time work.) We must also consider the nature of work itself. Various studies of work in technological society (for example, Special Task Force to the Secretary of Health, Education and Welfare, 1973) point to the paucity of opportunities for a person, through work, to sense that he or she exerts any meaningful impact on the environment. This lack extends from the assembly line to the paper-pushing bureaucracy in fields from agriculture to astronomy. An education that equips an individual for a life of work that precludes having any meaningful effect in the environment cannot be considered education for environmental competence. To be sure, it could be seen as education for economic survival. To make this point is not to suggest that the secondary school curriculum must reform the nature of work in modern society. That broader problem must be tackled by other institutions as well. The claim here is that career education, while it is indicative of a concern that education should be useful and directly applicable in students' lives, does not necessarily help students exert an impact on reality.

There are important qualifications to this survey on the ways in which schooling neglects environmental competence. Alternative schools, many publicly sponsored, often place students in roles where they learn to take responsibility, not only for individual choices, but also for collective action of the group. In struggling for their school's survival, students and staff learn to find and organize learning resources and to secure public support and funding. Those alternatives that emphasize the community beyond the school, for example, Parkway in Philadelphia or Metro in Chicago, involve students in numerous challenges to initiate action in the community-at-large and to cope with issues in the adult, nonschool world. The recent boom in school-sponsored volunteer programs presents further opportunities to develop environmental competence in helping others through tutoring, counseling, offering companionship, and taking care of dependent persons. Finally, numerous conventional in-school programs in the shop, laboratory, studio, darkroom, or on the athletic field promote activities requiring relatively high degrees of environmental control and manipulation. Such examples are welcome exceptions to the dominant thrust of major subjects in the secondary curriculum of most schools. Usually viewed as ancillary to the curriculum's major core, however, their existence does not modify the general contention that schools devote little attention to environmental competence.

Students do learn to play by the rules of the game, to adapt to demands that the school environment makes upon them, or, in short, to succeed in school. In this sense school develops abilities to function in bureaucratic structures that may be necessary in coping with adult life beyond the school. There is an important distinction, however, between learning to survive in an environment versus exerting some autonomous influence upon it. We could probably find students who more actively influence phenomena in the school environment to serve their own ends, an indication of more vigorous and self-assertive environmental competence. Such competence is gained, however, not necessarily because the curriculum intentionally tries to teach it. Some persons gain that mastery in spite of curriculum that, by and large, has different purposes.

Our concern with environmental competence is not an indictment of all that occurs in secondary school. When school succeeds in enhancing other forms of competence, it provides a valuable service, for other educational objectives are also justifiable, whether it be comprehension of aspects of the social and physical world, developing control over one's body, or gaining sensitivity to personal feelings. What concerns us is the relatively low priority, in contrast to other objectives, placed upon environmental competence, especially with regard to competence in public affairs.

Why would a curriculum be oriented rather exclusively toward passive forms of competence? This can be explained best, perhaps, by the general approach to socialization supported in the society-at-large, and characterized most dramatically by the segregation of youth from adults (Coleman, 1972a; Panel on Youth, 1974). For twelve, up to twenty, years or more of their lives (from kindergarten through high school or graduate school), youth are placed in special institutions, and adults structure a multitude of organizations and programs—church groups, Scouts, 4-H, municipal recreation, extracurricular clubs—to meet their alleged special needs. Youth also create their own separate groups—clubs, gangs, cliques. There are numerous explanations as to why youth in this society have been so conspicuously removed from participation in affairs of the adult world, but here the arguments are organized around three general orientations: technological, political-economic, and psychological. Rather than representing authentic and complete arguments of specific people, the orientations are caricatures used to illustrate salient points made in a variety of contexts.

The *technological* argument claims that, in contrast to previous historical periods when adult life seemed less complex, advanced industrial, technological societies require far more knowledge and sophisticated skills for adults to function successfully. Education, therefore, requires more time and effort than it has in the past. One of the characteristics of complex societies is specialization and division of labor. For the sake of technological efficiency, education is recognized as a special social function and delegated to separate institutions, rather than being integrated into the life of such institutions as the family, the workplace, or the church. Those to be educated are segregated from other institutions that produce goods, provide social services, enforce the law, conduct religious worship, or perform other functions. A pedagogical corollary of this view is that learning itself can be rationally subdivided into separate parts and organized into an efficient sequence. Rather than allowing youth to learn the competencies of citizenship through active practice and authentic responsibility, they must first master vast amounts of information and analysis, presumably so that they will "understand" society before they try to affect it.

Political-economic theories contend that system maintenance requires the isolation and subordination of youth. In contrast to earlier times, today's capitalistic economy could not tolerate the addition of youth to the labor force. Separate institutions are needed, therefore, to supervise and care for them. Preservation of the existing political and economic system also requires the inculcation of a sense of legitimacy and loyalty toward society's institutions, not serious questioning of them or active participation to change them. This view assumes that, in order to become a successfully functioning adult and also to preserve the political-economic system that itself supplies education, children must learn to accept or conform to the world as it is, rather than challenging or influencing it.

A *psychological* explanation for curriculum aimed more inward, toward development of self, than outward, toward affecting the environment assumes a gradual and systematically nurtured transition from youthful dependence to adult independence. By recognizing stages in cognitive and affective development, there is often an implication that experiences central to adult forms of exerting influence would be, for youth, either meaningless or possibly psychologically harmful. To ask students incapable of formal operational thought, for example, to debate the merits of alternative income maintenance plans could be inappropriate, or to give adolescents actual responsibility for distributing funds to real families could place too heavy an emotional burden on them. Finally, aspects of humanistic psychology can be interpreted as recommending that the key to personal growth is directing one's energy more toward inner examination of self, rather than toward making an impact in the external world.

Chapter 2 shows that many points in each of these positions are ill-founded, or disputable, if not clearly in error. They are raised here primarily to indicate that the lack of emphasis on environmental competence in secondary schools can be explained by conceptions of socialization in the society-at-large that influence, if only in subtle ways, what educators put into a curriculum.

Why Should the Schools Teach Environmental Competence?

Having defined environmental competence and claimed that schools make a relatively small investment in developing it, ethical and psychological theory can now be used to offer a rationale for environmental competence as an educational objective. Political theory is added to the rationale in Chapter 2, where this general objective is translated into the more specific notion of ability to exercise influence in public affairs.

Morality

The major proposition here is that the less ability one has to exert influence in the world, the more difficult it becomes to consider oneself a moral agent. A moral agent is defined as someone who deliberates upon what he or she ought to do in situations that involve possible conflicts between self-interests and the interests of others, or between the rights of parties in conflict. Some philosophers may require that a person deliberate only upon what ought to be done, but not necessarily upon what one, as an individual, ought to do. Unless our deliberations focus upon our own personal rights, duties, responsibilities, obligations—that is, what we ought to do—such deliberation is empty, academic, unrelated to the realities of our existence. We stipulate, therefore, that our moral nature derives from the existential necessity of deciding what we ought to do. Deliberating upon what ought to be done in a general sense and upon what others ought to do is important, but, unless this is supplemented by a concern for what I as an individual ought to do, I cannot properly be considered a moral agent.[10]

The less we are able to influence reality, the less we are able to deliberate about what we ought to do. Suppose that, while walking upon a deserted beach, I come upon a swimmer fifteen yards from shore who is calling for help. Nearby are a canoe and paddle, several loose strands of rope, and an automobile with keys in the ignition. I recognize as a general moral principle or prima facie duty that one should save a human life if this is at all possible. Suppose, however, that I do not know how to swim, manage a canoe, tie knots, or drive an auto. Nor do I have knowledge of where I might find the nearest person or telephone. Because of such overwhelming incompetence, it is meaningless to ask what I ought to do. Because I can do nothing to influence the situation, what I ought to do is not a genuine question.[11] If my incompetence prevents me from asking this question, it has in a sense deprived me of the essence of my nature as a moral agent.

10. This conception of moral agent depends upon the work of Hampshire (1959), Hare (1963), Frankena (1963), Baier (1965), and Wilson, Williams, and Sugarman (1967), although none presents an interpretation identical to the one presented here.

11. Hare (1963) provides a more thorough discussion of the point that "ought" implies "can." The converse, however, does not follow. That is, the possession of specific abilities to act (e.g., the ability to shoot or to type) does not imply what actions, if any, ought to be taken.

By way of contrast, suppose that I was highly skilled in lifesaving, canoeing, knot tying, driving, and that I knew how to summon help at this place. Thanks to these varied competencies to exert influence, I could choose to act in any of these ways, or not to act at all. Such competencies have created for me a choice among actions, and have thereby given birth to the important question: "What should I do?" Endowed with the ability to influence the environment, I am now capable of asking what I ought to do and therefore it is possible, albeit perhaps more stressful, to consider myself a moral agent. Such competencies are important not only because they help to make the important question "askable," but also because they make it possible for a person to act in accordance with ethical duties.

The claim that ability to exert influence is critical to our existence as moral agents should be interpreted with care. This does not require an individual to harbor specific intentions, make specific judgments, or act in specific ways that philosophers might consider morally correct. An extremely competent person in the above situation could conceivably choose *not* to help the drowning person for a variety of reasons—some, perhaps, selfish and immoral; others, ethically justifiable. Or, a totally incompetent person might make heroic attempts to save the swimmer, yet both could die in the process. Whether an individual wishes to attempt a rescue, actually attempts a rescue, or succeeds in rescuing the swimmer is not central to this argument, although such matters may be significant in making moral judgments of other types. We claim only that a critical and defining (perhaps necessary but not sufficient) feature of a moral agent is one's ability to deliberate about what one as an individual ought to do. The point of the swimmer analogy is to demonstrate that, to the extent that we lack the ability to influence the environment, we are also deprived of the chance to inquire about what we ought to do.[12]

We can further illustrate the ethical importance of environmental competence with reference to public issues. Imagine a student who, while studying reformatories and other institutions for "youthful of-

---

12. As mentioned earlier, the ability to exert influence is not simply a function of individual skills, knowledge, attitudes, etc. People can be limited by physical disabilities, economic deprivation, incarceration, and other factors. This concept of moral agent does not suggest that persons restricted by such factors are less "moral" than persons not so restricted. It does suggest, however, that, to the extent that such factors deprive a person of asking what one ought to do, they also limit one's opportunity to function as a moral agent.

fenders," concludes that reforms are needed and that she ought to be active in working toward certain policy changes. She writes a letter to a prison official and one to her congressman, requesting that they take whatever steps are necessary to implement her proposed policies, which include more licensed foster homes for offenders and runaways. Both letters are answered with the noncomittal: "Thank you for your interest. I will certainly consider your suggestions." The student concludes that nothing more can be done to advance her cause. She is unaware of other actions she might take; for example, finding and working with organizations that have already advocated similar policies, developing a new organization, working for the election of candidates who support her views. Her lack of knowledge of such approaches has rendered her powerless to act on what she considers to be her moral obligations.[13]

Recent events as varied as the knifing of Kitty Genovese in New York, the My Lai massacre, Watergate, or advertised sale of term papers on college campuses seem to have triggered a widespread sense of moral outrage and a renewed interest in "moral education." To cure the moral pathology allegedly plaguing our civilization, different educational prescriptions are offered for youth: more effective inculcation of certain substantive values such as honesty, respect for life, constitutional rights; direct analysis of students' confusion over personal values and helping them identify the values to which they are genuinely committed (Raths, Harmin, and Simon, 1966); cultivation of better structures within which to carry on moral deliberation, advancing, for example, from hedonistic orientation and conventional obedience to law to principled reasoning based on a philosophically adequate conception of justice (Kohlberg, 1969, 1971).[14] An approach to moral and values education as they relate to public issues has also been advocated (Newmann and Oliver, 1970), and it is further developed in Chapter 3, largely in agreement with Kohlberg's philosophical position. It is possible, however, that even the more sophisticated attempts to clarify the nature of moral discourse

---

13. Even with more sophisticated knowledge of techniques of exerting influence, one might still have chosen to drop the matter if one felt, for example, that it would involve too much work or self-sacrifice. The point remains that, without such knowledge, the option to pursue certain convictions was not as readily available to the student.

14. See Kohlberg and Mayer (1972) for a critique of the inculcation or "bag of virtues" approach, and Lockwood (in press) for a critique of the "values clarification" approach.

appropriate for schools have missed the mark, for they do not give adequate attention to the ethical implications of student incompetence to exert influence in their environment.

We can illustrate the point by a review of the kinds of ethical issues often presented in values-oriented curricula. One case (used in Kohlberg's research) tells of a man who, in order to save his wife from a fatal disease, must steal a wonder drug because he cannot afford to pay for it. Another is the classical lifeboat situation in which the lives of some people must apparently be sacrificed if anyone is to survive. When considering matters of public policy, students may be asked to evaluate the morality of Truman's decision to use the atomic bomb or to decide whether a soldier who killed innocent civilians under orders from a superior officer should be morally condemned. While each of these situations raises fundamental ethical issues of universal significance and while each may assist students in arriving at clearer and consistent statements of the abstract principles on which to base ethical choices, these subjects of moral discourse are insufficient as a basis for moral education. In each situation the individual whose actions are being evaluated *does* have the ability to act in ways that exert important influence in the environment. The decision maker's problem lies not in the attainment of the ability to exert influence, but in choosing how one's rather considerable power ought to be used. Because the decision maker is assumed to have enough environmental competence to make a dramatic difference, discourse restricted to "what should be done" can neglect the basic point that "real" moral dilemmas exist only for those persons who have specific abilities to affect reality.

This is particularly important when we consider the actual or perceived incompetence of young people to exert influence in their own lives. They may have a sense of injustice with regard to many topics: environmental decay, economic exploitation of certain groups, violations of constitutional rights, or international violence. Because they do not consider themselves capable of action to remedy such injustices, they, in effect, face no actual moral dilemmas. The challenge for moral education is not simply to improve the process of reasoned verification of ethical choices, but also to build competence to affect the environment so that authentic ethical choices will actually present themselves to students.

At times the study of values in schools can raise situations of crucial personal relevance: Should a girl have a right to an abortion? Should a student be failed for cheating? Should a person divulge information about a close friend's pushing of heroin? Such situations, in which students do have the ability to act, may appear more authentic, and they can raise serious, complicated ethical choices.[15] Even these cases, however, like those more exotic and distant from the students' experience, may provide no help in expanding competence to act in areas where students are currently impotent. Though students may benefit from guided reflection on such choices, there is an additional challenge: expanding students' horizons for action so that problems that beset them now only academically can be transformed, through increased ability to act, into authentic ethical dilemmas. Moral education on how to reason about ethical choices will then become even more appropriate, for students will be able to see themselves as moral agents.

Psychological Development

Just as the ability to affect the environment is critical to one's identity as a moral agent, so is it central to fulfilling a fundamental psychological need. Robert White (1959, 1960, 1963, 1973), who reviewed a wide range of research in the psychoanalytic tradition, in empirical studies of animal and human behavior, and in cognitive psychological theory, has identified a persistent human tendency, beginning in early childhood, to explore, manipulate, and exert impact upon one's environment. White explains how findings of numerous studies suggest that this behavior cannot be construed merely as a form of coping with more basic instinctual drives (sex, food, aggression, and so forth). Instead, this seems to constitute a bundle of independent ego energies which he labels *effectance*. To try to act upon the environment and to derive satisfaction therefrom is a basic element in human nature that is also apparent in other animals. In humans, this form of satisfaction can be called a *feeling of efficacy*:

My thesis is that the feeling of efficacy is a primitive biological endowment as basic as the satisfactions that accompany feeding or sexual gratification, though not nearly as intense. We are most familiar with the feeling of efficacy at a level of behavior where we act with intentions to produce particular effects. We feel efficacious when we throw the ball over the plate, swim to the raft, or mend the broken household appliance. But the feeling does not have to be connected with the achievement of a particular intended result. With exploratory behavior, where results cannot be anticipated, it seems a better guess to say that feelings of

---

15. Leming (1973) compared adolescents' reactions to "classical" versus actual personal moral dilemmas.

efficacy accompany the whole process of producing effects. The activity is satisfying in itself, not for specific consequences [White, 1963, page 35].

White claims no originality in recognizing effectance as a psychic phenomenon, and he acknowledges many other investigators who have been intrigued with its manifestations. White's contribution is his insistence that action or manipulative and exploratory behavior be regarded not simply as playful use of superfluous energy or expression of leisure curiosity in one's surroundings, but as a "major aspect of the adaptive process and a vital theme in the growth of personality." Effectance, especially in young children, is not consciously purposeful or instrumental. Their early actions upon the world are undertaken unintentionally, not in order to learn useful skills or to prepare for future contingencies but because there is something inherently satisfying about them.

At the same time, noninstrumental behavior involving assertive, exploratory interaction with the environment stimulates cognitive development and also produces substantive knowledge, however "accidentally." White's work is thus consistent with cognitive developmental theory, particularly the research of Piaget (1937) and others on the growth of cognitive complexity in children. The child's earliest conception of causality, for example, emerges not through passive observation and reflection, but from feelings associated with specific actions on concrete phenomena in the environment. Similarly, Dewey (1916, 1938), in his explanation of cognitive growth, argues that reconstruction of experience occurs only through the person's active intervention or interaction with people and objects in the environment. Whether we look at growth through Piaget's notion of cognitive complexity, through Dewey's "reconstruction of experience," or through Kohlberg's (1971) stages in the development of moral reasoning, there is wide agreement that development is generated, in large part, through perception of dissonance, inconsistency, mystery, or other ways of experiencing intellectual inadequacy and that the personal sense of such inadequacy arises from our attempts to influence and confront reality external to self. Our effectance needs apparently have evolutionary value. White reminds us that, while the pursuit of effectance is intrinsically satisfying, the concomitant learning it brings about can make the difference between life and death for an organism or species.[16]

---

16. Rosen (1974) makes a fascinating, concise argument for the biologically intrinsic value of environmental competence.

As the individual grows, it is hoped that the exercise of effectance and feelings of efficacy will be directed toward specific kinds of mastery so that *competence* and a *sense of competence* are developed. These are, respectively, the actual ability to bring about specific results in one's environment and the sense that one can bring about such results consistently.[17] Though many of White's illustrations deal with the physical world, he emphasizes the equal significance of social or interpersonal efficacy—the ability to act toward persons in such a way that elicits human responses in accordance with one's intentions. In a further modification of psychoanalytic theory, White explains how children's attempts to identify with adults can be seen not merely as incorporating the person of the adult into oneself, but copying the competence of others in order to improve one's own competence. Competence also constitutes the foundation of self-esteem based on self-respect, in contrast, for example, to self-love, as particular standards for mastery in the environment become internalized criteria for one's self-esteem. Finally, White indicates how an accumulated sense of competence is a useful way of referring to what others may call ego-strength—the ability to overcome anxiety associated with perceived "dangers" or "threats," because of the accrued confidence that one can act upon, rather than be a victim of, the environment.

The psychological significance of environmental competence is evident in many other works, although, until now, the two specific words have not been joined. Edrita Fried (1970), on the basis of her clinical practice in psychotherapy and scholarly inquiries, posits the need for "activeness" as the "crucial psychological dimension." She argues that the major dynamic in human personality is not tension reduction or the pursuit of hedonistic pleasure in a passive sense, but a vital and active desire to affect reality. Passivity occurs essentially as a defensive reaction to the blocking of or failure to nurture the active need. Smith (1968), drawing from biological, psychological, and sociological studies, contributes a major synthesis in the study of competence. He recommends that the concept of a competent self orient our thinking about socialization from youth to adulthood. The core of the competent self is the ability to act in one's environment:

---

17. Recall our earlier point that White's notion of competence is equivalent to our "environmental competence."

The self is perceived as causally important, as effective in the world—which is to a major extent a world of other people—as likely to be able to bring about desired effects, and as accepting responsibility when effects do not correspond to desire [page 281].

Coleman's (Coleman *et al.*, 1966) finding that a sense of control over one's environment and future seems to have a stronger relationship to school achievement than all other "school" factors (for example, dollars per pupil, education of teachers) together should further alert us to the significance of this need.

A concern for the psychological potency of environmental competence is present in Erikson's conception of identity formation (1959, 1968). His stages of autonomy, initiative, industry, identity, intimacy, generativity, and integrity all presume a person who acts upon reality, rather than passively observing or merely understanding it. Maslow's (1954) ideal of self-actualization also implies the ability of an individual to affect reality in accord with intentions. In short, most of our conceptions of psychological health, mental health, or functional personality development, expressed in professional or lay language, rely upon this notion. Perhaps this seems so obvious that it need not be mentioned. It is possible, however, that, in paying so much attention to complex derivatives or facets of competence such as advanced cognitive operations that make up "critical thinking," stages in the development of moral reasoning, or affective education aimed at self-awareness, we may have lost sight of the central task of helping individuals exert purposeful impact in their own environment.

Qualifications

An ethical and psychological case for environmental competence as a general educational goal has been made, but further qualifications are needed. Many manifestations of environmental competence may be irrelevant from an ethical or psychological point of view. These cannot be enumerated in advance, for they depend upon the idiosyncracies of unique situations. Teaching a young child to make his bed may be powerfully responsive to a child's effectance needs, yet it may be contrary to the needs of an adolescent. The ability to make one's bed could conceivably have ethical significance (creating responsibilities for sharing in the work of maintaining a household), but, conversely, it may never in a given life be construed as enhancing one's identity as a moral agent. To learn how to ride the subway or how to organize a car wash may seem trivial to some persons, but it may introduce others to exciting new forms of competence, with ethical implications. In endorsing environmental competence as a general goal, we are not, therefore, arguing that all forms of environmental competence are equally significant for all youth in all situations.

Dewey (1938), in his analysis of growth makes it clear that not all experiences with the environment should be considered educational. He argues, for example, that, in selecting experiences, the educator must follow the principles of continuity (connecting the present with past and future experiences in a way that "arouses curiosity, strengthens initiative, and sets up desires and purposes") and interaction (being sensitive to the ways in which external conditions and internal states of mind in the learner combine to yield an "experience"). Developmental theory suggests that experiences be designed consistently with the cognitive stage of the learner so that the learner experiences an appropriate type of dissonance. Development is unlikely to occur if the problems (moral dilemmas or interaction with physical phenomena) can be adequately resolved through stages of thinking "lower" than the learner's level, or if the problems require stages of thought so far beyond the learner that no genuine dissonance is perceived. It is not possible to give specific prescriptions on how to match learners with experiences so that meaningful environmental competence results. This requires extensive future research. Once aware of the need to deliberate carefully about the types of environmental competence appropriate for different individuals, and with developmental theory already providing some rough guidelines, we can, nevertheless, avoid unconditional endorsement of all forms of action as educational.

There is a danger that our definition of environmental competence might be interpreted as implying an arrogant, if not immoral, form of individualism. Are we not suggesting that each individual should learn how to exert any impact on the world that he or she wishes? Does this place individual self-interest above concern for the rights of others, superior to the value of cooperation or justice for mankind in general? Does it imply that man is above nature, able to control it according to his will, rather than part of an ecologically interdependent system? Chapter 2 explains that all attempts to exert influence in the world are properly subject to moral deliberation, that no action derives ethical legitimacy from the fact that a person wishes it to occur. Its moral justification must be based upon other considerations, such as whether intentions surrounding it, its nature, and its consequences are consistent with the values of justice, equality, or human dignity. In arguing that we should assist students in effecting their intended consequences in the world, we are thus assuming that such actions would be preceded by moral deliberation, and that educators are in no sense bound to assist students in the commission of immoral acts. This qualification is issued with the full realization that some actions may be widely agreed to be immoral; others, moral; and the morality of many other actions may be in dispute among responsible observers.

In addition to the ethical provision, there are logical and empirical qualifications to our conception of individuals exerting impact in the world. Assuming that individuals often have intentions directly contradictory to one another, it is logically impossible for everyone to be successful in imposing their will, even if it were ethically justifiable. Furthermore, we are increasingly impressed with the view that the earth (or the universe) is a closed biological system with limited resources, and that human actions have complex multivariate effects throughout the system, effects that eventually turn back upon the actor. This perspective, applied to social as well as physical phenomena, informs us that the exercise of influence should not be viewed as a one-way process that terminates when the actor has affected the audience. Rather, the exercise of influence should be seen as an interactive or synergetic process in which actors and audience inevitably affect each other in multitudinous ways. According to this view, one cannot act *upon* the world; one acts only *within* it. The vision of an isolated individual unilaterally influencing others has been persuasively refuted even as a political strategy by thinkers as "revolutionary" as Freire (1970). It has also been rejected as detrimental to psychological growth.[18] For all of these reasons our conception of environmental competence assumes that, to fulfill one's intentions, one must view oneself as an interdependent part of the

---

18. Hampden-Turner's (1970) model of "radical man," in outlining a conception of growth based on interaction and synergy, contains an intriguing synthesis of the work of Maslow, Rogers, Erikson, and others.

physical and human environment, not standing above and apart from it as a totally independent agent.

Summary

Having assumed that competence, or the ability to engage in behavior to produce the consequences one intends, is a central goal of education, a distinction was made between intentions aimed primarily at making an impact in the environment external to oneself versus those aimed more clearly inward, toward comprehension of the environment or development of personal sensitivities. In drawing a further distinction between goals and activities, it has been shown that activities, regardless of the ends they may serve, involve higher and lower degrees of manipulation and control of environmental contingencies external to self. Conventional schooling has placed relatively little emphasis on helping students make an impact in the environment, and there are alternative explanations for this tendency.[19] In arguing that environmental competence should be given far more attention in secondary curricula, the rationale did not depend upon a utilitarian socialization argument that such competence will help an individual perform specific adult roles. Rather, the case was built on the grounds that environmental competence is needed to establish our identity as moral agents and to fulfill a fundamental psychological need.

This general rationale does not allow us to conclude that all forms of environmental competence would be equally legitimate as educational objectives. If schools were to educate for all forms of "action," they could be put in the position of supporting immoral acts, trivial acts, and acts that might inhibit rather than enhance the learning of environmental competence itself. There remains, then, much room for debate on the particular forms of environmental competence that ought to be promoted. The remaining portion of this book develops the case for one manifestation of environmental

---

19. Nisbet (1973) notes in our society an "obsessive concern with self" which, from a sociological and historical point of view, is an indication of decadence in civilization. Slater (1970) is equally critical of individualism that has taken the form of antisocial privatism. To the extent that social problems originate from the lack of a cooperative or collectivist ethic (a belief shared by many, especially in the Marxist tradition), excessive attention to self-oriented competence in schools may, in large part, cause and exacerbate those problems.

competence—namely, the ability to exercise influence in public affairs. As one form of environmental competence, the ability to exert influence in public affairs, has already been partially justified here. Chapter 2 uses political theory to demonstrate why this type of environmental competence should be honored with more commitment in public education.

CHAPTER 2
Exerting Influence in Public Affairs

Definition of the Objective

Environmental competence must now be translated into a more specific form. The ability to exert influence in public affairs, one facet of our ability to affect the world around us, is the more specific educational objective that will occupy us through the rest of this book. Public affairs are those issues of concern to groups of people to which, it is generally agreed, institutions of government should respond—through legislation, administrative action, judicial opinion, and other activities. Sometimes it is difficult to distinguish between private and public affairs. A student may feel that a parent has unjustly denied him or her use of the family car. Though this appears to be a private dispute within a family, the problem could escalate into a public issue if the student attempted to challenge the constitutionality of regulations that deny certain rights to "minors," and that give parents powers to restrict the "liberty" of children "without due process of law." Rather than classifying issues categorically as either private or public, it is more helpful to view them on a continuum. A problem can be regarded as "public" when increasing numbers of people become concerned with its resolution and when it is interpreted as falling within the realm of governmental interests. To the extent that a problem is viewed as idiosyncratic to individuals, rather than groups, and to the extent that it is not deemed to fall within governmental interests, it should be considered private.[1]

---

1. Much of the business of public affairs consists in determining which matters should be resolved through governmental channels. An unemployed person living in poverty might

There may be a tendency to identify public affairs as being only those issues of widespread significance usually depicted in the mass media (wars, elections, inflation, pollution, and other societal "crises"). Our definition expands the conception to include countless additional issues, more local in nature and less likely to receive media coverage. Cyclists may wish to establish and assist in the regulation of bike trails. Volunteer workers may wish to change some regulations in a mental hospital. Housing organizers may seek more frequent trash collection or more frequent inspection for code violations. Students may advocate an increased budget for women's athletics at the high school. A center for runaways may attempt to influence policies in a police department or a juvenile court. A black student union may have to work for official recognition by the school. According to our definition, these are all attempts to exert influence in public affairs. Though some may be considered "more public" than others, the citizens' ability to take action upon them is no less important than their ability to exert influence on issues with more global effects.

What does it mean to exert influence? This can be viewed as a process (Figure 1) in which the individual develops some goals or desired outcomes in public affairs (a strong antipollution ordinance, the closing of a juvenile detention center). The goals should be formulated through a rational process of social research and moral deliberation described in Chapter 3. One then works to develop support for the goals by persuading, organizing, and bargaining with people in appropriate groups, organizations, institutions—activity that will also be described further in Chapter 3. In seeking support, one often finds it necessary to modify original goals (lowering some of the pollution standards in the ordinance, hiring a new director instead of closing a center entirely). The revised goals serve as a new basis for action that could eventually call for even further revision as the campaign proceeds. One major problem for an activist is the extent to which one

---

face a number of "personal" problems (poor diet, no recreation, or marital conflict), not recognized as public issues by the public-at-large. If the person were to advocate that public agencies help with these troubles, then heretofore private issues would enter the public arena. Often public policies are promoted precisely to deter government from encroachment on private life (e.g., prohibitions on electronic eavesdropping or legal protection of the confidentiality of doctor-patient relationships). The struggle in approving or opposing such policies is, of course, a public affair.

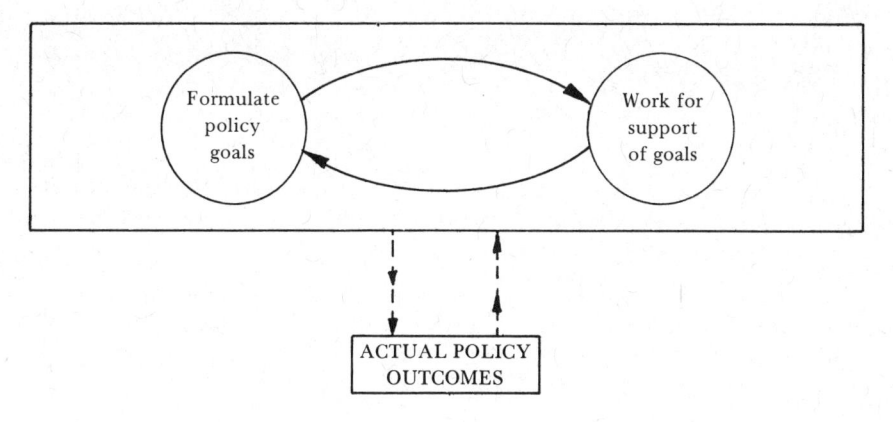

FIGURE 1
Exerting influence in public affairs

can tolerate continual modification of goals. If, in order to muster support, one must forsake basic principles, the loss of personal integrity may be considered too high a price for the successful exercise of influence.

A person can be said to exert influence when one's actions affect the outcomes of public affairs in a direction consistent with one's goals. As an example, consider Bob, a student who wants official bicycle routes established in his city. He joins a group of cyclists who, together with various environmentalist groups, have been trying to persuade businessmen, educators, aldermen, and officials in the city's traffic, recreation, and planning offices to support the idea. For about six months Bob helps conduct research on students' preferences for bike routes and their predicted frequency of travel; he organizes testimony for some public hearings; he solicits private donations to be used for signs, paving, and other necessary aspects. After two years a plan is adopted by the city traffic and recreation departments. It includes only 70 percent of the mileage in bike trails originally advocated by Bob and his associates, and it is contingent on the raising of twice the proportion of private funds initially proposed.

Did Bob's actions affect public policy in a direction consistent with his goals? In studying his role in this issue, we might conclude (*a*) that the same policy would have resulted if Bob had never been involved, so he exerted no influence; (*b*) that he did affect the outcome, but in a direction opposite from his intentions, perhaps because he antagonized people and produced a backlash against bike trails, which is reflected in the lower level of public funding and the cut in mileage; (*c*) that he was indispensable to the effort and that without his participation no bike trails would have been approved; or (*d*) that, because his efforts were so intertwined with others', Bob's individual effect is impossible to assess, but that the general "movement" did lead to the city's adoption of bike trails consistent with Bob's aims. It is also possible that Bob's own sense of the effect of his actions would differ from the conclusions of an impartial observer. Here we see how difficult it can be to assess the precise effect of an individual's actions. This problem continues to trouble activists, historians, and social scientists who wish to evaluate the impact of individuals and groups on public policy. Although there remain great difficulties in the empirical assessment of the exercise of influence, we need not await resolution of such uncertainties in order further to define and justify philosophically this educational objective.

While the concept may suggest that each student should learn how to impose all his or her views on the world, this is not our intent. Such an interpretation would be indefensible for two major reasons. As noted in Chapter 1, it would be ethically irresponsible to endorse unconditionally any view on public affairs that a student might profess. If a student wishes to bomb a building to protest a war, the teacher is not obligated to help, even though the student may believe this will increase his or her ability to win support. In such cases the teacher may, instead, be morally obligated to make it impossible for the student to implement his views. Rather than giving a blank check to students to exercise their will as they see fit, we must assume that study and discussion on the ethics of the policies one supports and on the actions one takes is a moral responsibility of students and staff. Instruction in moral deliberation is discussed again in Chapter 3.

Such deliberation might well result in conflict between school and students over policies and methods of action that the school is willing to support. It is also possible that school authorities, under the guise of "moral" objections, will prohibit student projects for other reasons (for example, to maintain adult authority or to avoid inconveniences within a bureaucracy). The way in which schools may use their power in politically biased or neutral ways is discussed further below, and measures to minimize arbitrary censorship by school authorities or community groups in selection of student projects are discussed in Chapter 4. The concern here is that the goal of generally increasing one's ability to exert influence does not require the school to support every policy or action preferred by a student.

There is another reason why we must not equate exerting influence with the right to win or to implement one's views unilaterally at all times. A social system could not function on such a premise, for it would have to guarantee that persons with contradictory views could each have their way. Genuine controversy over public affairs inevitably spawns "winners," "losers," and people who see themselves as being somewhere between; it is impossible to have only winners. Thus, a conception of the ability to exercise influence should recognize (a) the impossibility of all citizens winning *all* of the time, but the desirability of all "winning" *some* of the time; (b) the fact that, in the process of "losing," even "losers" can exert influence on policy (for example, by demonstrating a power base that will have to be contended with in the future); and (c) that the necessity of modifying one's ideals in order to exert influence in a particular situation is not, ipso facto, an indication of one's lack of ability to exert influence. Having one's way is surely implied in the concept of influence outlined here, but it cannot be taken to the extreme as an exclusive criterion for defining the concept. The goal is to assist students in having some impact in public affairs, consistent with intentions which they develop through a process of rational and moral deliberation.

As another point of clarification, note that the objective is not to make all students into adults obsessed with public affairs who participate intensively and continuously on every conceivable issue. Exclusive preoccupation with civic matters would leave no time for other significant roles, responsibilities, and satisfactions in life. Rather than prescribing for all students a standard style or expected frequency of actual involvement, the objective is concerned mainly with increasing the ability to exert influence. Each individual must retain choice as to where, when, and how he or she wishes to use competence in an area, and some may choose to use it only infrequently. Without possessing certain skills, however, the individual does not have the option to choose to exert influence. If a person is incompetent, the only options are not to participate or to participate without effect. The school should create for all students another option: to participate in a way that makes an impact. Even if this objective were achieved, there would be wide variation in rates and types of actual participation among those who received such instruction.

Justification of the Objective: Consent of the Governed

As a form of environmental competence, the ability to exert influence in public affairs has already been justified as an educational objective through ethical and psychological arguments presented in Chapter 1. Theory on the nature of citizen participation in democracy provides additional, and especially significant, rationale from a political perspective.

We begin with the assumption that state-supported, publicly financed education ought to work for the maintenance and enhancement of democratic political process. While there may be some dispute about the defining characteristics of a democratic system, the principle of consent of the governed is a central requirement, and there is little doubt that, as an *ideal,* this is well established in American culture. Numerous legal provisions are made to give each citizen the right to influence the course of public affairs: universal suffrage; periodic election of officials for relatively short terms; electoral districts drawn presumably to give each person equal proportional representation; the use of majority rule to resolve public disagreement; protection of freedom of political expression and the right of assembly; opportunity for citizen-initiated petitions, referenda, and recall; public access to government meetings and records. The attention paid to many surveys of public opinion (not required by law) endows the "will of the people" with further dignity.

This is not to say that the consent ideal has been sufficiently realized (Newmann, 1963). A major reason for this book is the belief that it is not fulfilled, and that education is, in part, responsible for its failure. In spite of evidence that many citizens do not actually participate extensively or effectively in their government, we must recognize, nevertheless, an emotionally powerful consensus that we ought to have this right. So much of the rhetoric in public discourse extols the virtue of the consent ideal that few would dare to attack it.

On what grounds is the consent ideal a justifiable political principle? Without discussing numerous complications in political philosophy or delineating the sophisticated contributions of seminal thinkers on this subject, we summarize two powerful routes of justification. From an ethical point of view, the consent principle is a mechanism for the realization of a central value in theories of morality and justice: the value of equality. We assume that the general moral significance of equality has been adequately demonstrated (Vlastos, 1962; Scriven, 1966; Kohlberg, 1971; Rawls, 1971), and here we outline how the consent principle can be seen as a device for institutionalizing equality in political matters.[2]

A basic moral premise is that every human being, because of one's humanity, is entitled to respect and dignity. That dignity is possible only if the claims and interests of each person are treated impartially, that is, given equal consideration. It is a social fact, however, that some persons who might gain power over others might also subjugate or deny equal rights to the powerless. To guard against this possibility, it would be helpful to organize society through a political principle that disperses and distributes power itself as equally as possible. Consent of the governed serves this purpose, for it requires that each citizen should have equal opportunity to affect the use of power, both through periodic selection of leaders and through direct participation to affect the outcome of specific issues. By emphasizing equal access to power, the consent principle minimizes the likelihood that equal rights, the cornerstone of morality and justice, can be violated. Consent of the governed, therefore, has an ethical foundation.

The consent principle can also be justified as a means of ferreting out the "truth," or compensating for errors in judgment. Others (such as Dewey, 1916; Thorson, 1962) have developed this argument more carefully. For many questions of public policy, there is often genuine dispute that cannot be attributed to political bias alone, for even the most impartial experts will disagree. Thus, solutions objectively verified beyond doubt can rarely be found. We also learn through hindsight that in science and in public affairs men have often

---

2. Some authors recognize justice as the central principle of morality and, in turn, equality as the central principle of justice. Others will link morality and equality more directly.

held up as sacred truths claims later proved wrong. Realizing our inability to find eternally valid answers to questions on public affairs (or scientific matters), we must guard against becoming victimized by adherence to mistaken orthodoxies. One safeguard is to provide equal opportunity for all citizens continuously to advocate solutions as they see fit. If the power to influence policy is widely dispersed among the citizenry, there is more likely to be a "sifting and winnowing" of ideas, an experimentation with alternative proposals, an openness and constructive struggle for the "right" answers. Such a process would not be possible if power were restricted to a special group. In this sense the justification for consent of the governed is similar to arguments for academic freedom and freedom of speech: it tries to maximize our opportunity to arrive at the "truest" or "wisest" decisions, however temporary these may be.[3]

Having justified the consent ideal ethically and epistemologically, we can inquire about the extent to which it has been achieved. Systematic empirical assessment of citizens' actual ability to exert influence in public affairs has not been undertaken, but studies of political behavior shed some light on the topic. Since the 1950's, social scientists have accumulated data on rates of political participation (frequency of attending political functions, making financial contributions to campaigns, and so forth), political interest (frequency of reading and discussion on public affairs), political knowledge (mastery of information on issues and the governing process), political efficacy (the feeling that one can exert impact on the government), and, more recently, government responsiveness to political participation. Findings of the studies differ somewhat over time, but they are often difficult to compare because of variation in the survey questions. A brief review of the literature follows.

Several sources have found relatively low levels of participation in public affairs (Campbell *et al.*, 1954; Almond and Verba, 1963; Milbrath, 1965; Robinson *et al.*, 1968).[4] The majority does not partici-

---

3. In spite of general positive regard for the consent ideal, some would balk at the prospect of every citizen armed with actual ability to make an impact in public affairs. Would this lead to such massive and continuous participation that no stable policies could be made? Would public policy be formulated more impulsively, less rationally? Fears related to predictions of "excessive" participatory democracy are discussed below.

4. Studies on political behavior usually deal with a conception of politics concentrating on electoral participation (participation in campaigns, letters to legislators, etc.). Our definition is broader, including, for example, trying to get more frequent visits from a housing inspector, meeting with neighbors to make complaints about abandoned cars in the neigh-

pate regularly in the nomination and election of officials, nor does it try to exert influence on specific issues. In 1966, 84 percent of the Americans sampled reported that they had *never* tried to influence a local government decision (Schwartz, 1973, page 14). Verba and Nie (1972) construed citizen action more broadly than studies which focused only on electoral politics. They asked, for example, whether a person had "ever worked with others in trying to solve some community problems," and their results indicate more widespread participation than earlier studies. But, even so, they conclude that active involvement is not sustained, and that

1. Few, if any, types of political activity beyond the act of voting are performed by more than a third of the American citizenry.
2. Activities that require the investment of more than trivial amounts of time . . . tend to be performed by no more than 10 to 15 percent of the citizens.
3. Less demanding activities . . . are performed by between 15 and 30 percent of the citizenry [page 32].

The authors (pages 118-119) identify distinct types of participation as follows:

Type	Percent	Participation
Inactive	22	No activity
Voting specialist	21	Vote regularly, but do nothing else
Parochial participant	4	Contact local officials on particular personal problems, but are otherwise inactive
Communalist	20	Contact officials on broad issues and engage in cooperative group activity, vote fairly regularly, but avoid election campaigns
Campaigner	15	Heavily active in campaigns and vote regularly
Complete activist	11	Active in all ways
Unclassified	7	
	100	

borhood, persuading a school to cut down on energy consumption, or establishing a counseling center for runaways. As seen in the study by Verba and Nie (1972), a broader definition could inflate rates of participation. "Low" is obviously a relative term. Almond and Verba (1963) show, for example, that citizen participation in the United States is considerably higher than in other countries.

According to this breakdown, 11 percent of the citizenry is extremely active and 47 percent (inactives, voting specialists, parochials) is relatively inactive.[5] In contrast to the image of the activist as a young radical, Verba and Nie find that the high participators are overwhelmingly upper-status, wealthy, white, middle-aged citizens, taking a "conservative" stand on such issues as welfare.

Low rates of participation alone might not indicate citizen impotence, for conceivably many individuals could view themselves as capable of acting effectively, but deliberately choose not to participate. Studies of political efficacy, however, tend to refute this interpretation. Schwartz (1973, page 236), in reviewing data presented in Robinson *et al.* (1968), observed that 52.5 percent of those who reported an opinion believed, in 1966, that they would fail in any effort to influence a local governmental decision, and 70.7 percent believed that any effort they might make to affect the Congress would come to nothing. In the same study, 61 percent believed that politicians could not help them (or would hurt them) in seeking governmental redress of grievance. The Verba and Nie (1972, page 370) data indicate a higher sense of efficacy, but also leave much room for improvement. In asking, "How much influence do you think people like you can have over local government?", 17.3 percent answered "a lot"; 35.2 percent, "moderate." The remaining 47.5 percent indicated "not so well" (27.4), "not at all" (18.1), and "don't know" (2.0). From this we conclude that feelings of political efficacy in the citizenry at large have been relatively low.

Is it possible that persons misjudge their efficacy and feel relatively powerless, but, in fact, possess great competence to exert influence? No studies have measured actual competence, and, of the data available, surveys of citizen knowledge about public affairs seem most likely to offer some clues. Unfortunately, many of the tests of knowledge ask persons only to name official leaders at various levels of government; they do not probe one's understanding of particular issues or channels of influence. There are also studies, however, which show that "few citizens know what they want. They do not

---

5. The increased rates of participation found here may be due in part to the fact that on Verba and Nie's (1972, pp. 351-353) questionnaire six of the twelve items on participation asked whether the person had "ever" performed the act and two of the twelve asked whether an act had been performed within the last three or four years. The authors themselves note that increasing the time referent can increase participation figures.

have clear and consistent positions on the important issues of the day.... Very few respondents (3.5 percent of voters) could be considered to have a political ideology of a clear sort..." (Verba and Nie, 1972, page 104). Even the naming of one's elected representatives poses problems for most citizens, and their mastery of information on more complicated matters is probably much worse (Campbell et al., 1954; Berelson et al., 1954; Matthews and Prothro, 1966; Robinson, 1967; Robinson et al., 1968). Personal observations of youth and adults, including those actively involved in public affairs, further reveals to this author a striking incompetence in the exercise of influence.

Some may contend that failure to participate or to develop personal competence in public affairs is a reasonable human reaction to a mammoth system that is itself incapable of responding rationally to citizen action. This conclusion might be drawn from a number of perspectives, some of which were discussed in the Introduction. Does the political-economic system require exploitation of the masses? Does the cult of technology and meritocracy bestow uncontestable authority in a class of "experts"? Does centralization of power and long-term planning by agencies and corporations preclude any possibility for local and short-term citizen input? Is the macrosystem so complex that outcomes in public affairs are beyond the control of human beings? Is human civilization headed toward inevitable destruction? In the face of conclusive affirmative answers to all these questions, characterized henceforth as the "gloomy assessment," anyone who tried to develop personal competence to exert influence would seem insane.

If we accept, for the sake of argument, the belief that the system by its nature represses citizen involvement, consent of the governed *as an ideal* can still remain untarnished, for even the system's harshest critics depend upon it as a value that lends weight to their criticism. The implicit, if not explicit, goal of many such critiques is to change the system so as to allow for increased citizen control. If there is any hope for deliberate efforts to move the system itself close to the consent ideal, such efforts cannot be successful unless individuals have ability to exert influence.

We do not agree with the gloomy assessment, but must recognize that, for many who accept it, the only sensible reaction is to drop out. Rather than wasting time on public policy, one can invest oneself in more private matters: arts, crafts, hobbies, sports, meditation, interpersonal relations, family, for example. Realizing the dangers of oversimplification, a distinction between communal and individualistic dropouts can be made. Communal dropouts try to fulfill the consent ideal in small, local, "manageable" groups, sometimes believed to operate "outside" the system, as in communes which deliberately segregate themselves from straight society. Here, personal energies may be directed toward the organization of a local craft or food cooperative, a neighborhood day-care center or health clinic, an organic farm, or a parent-run school, but not toward changing the local university, the auto industry, or the Defense Department. Even those who choose to ignore the "macro" issues, working instead on local community projects, inevitably take part in public affairs. In governing themselves, they operate a consent system that makes and maintains community norms and handles conflict resolution. Moreover, to implement their plans they often must confront policies of the establishment; for example, on licensing, building facilities, taxes, or the care of minors. For these reasons efforts to "make a difference" or to take control of one's life at a local community level do not constitute withdrawal from civic life. To be successful in their endeavors, even communal dropouts need personal competence to exert influence in public affairs.

Individualistic dropouts turn more noticeably to private activity in the form of hobbies, recreation, family life, or attempts to grow in self-awareness. Most of one's personal competence might be channeled into caring for a garden or a child, rebuilding a car or making jewelry, demonstrating physical prowess in the streets or on the golf course. Once basic subsistence and some leisure activity are assured, who needs to worry about civic issues? Is it possible that most people can totally neglect public issues yet still fulfill psychological needs for effectance and competence? No doubt it is possible to achieve a sense of personal efficacy without continuously struggling with global policy issues, and many people may feel content in the life styles implied here.

We suggest, however, that exclusive investment in private, individualistic forms of efficacy is not sufficient for most people. It is virtually impossible to insulate oneself from the constant flow of information on public affairs across the planet. We are bombarded with messages and images that evoke strong feelings of justice and injustice. In spite of a sense of powerlessness, the messages can never be entirely blocked out, and many people hold strong views on selected social problems. Commitment to private individual endeavors may offer temporary relief, but for most people, including adolescents, this does not resolve an underlying frustration that the consent ideal remains unfulfilled. Rawls (1971, page 84) speaks to this problem when he claims that those deprived of positions of power in society would rightfully feel unjustly treated even though they were to gain great benefits from the efforts of a privileged few. They would be justified in their complaint not only because they were excluded from external rewards of wealth and privilege, "but because they were debarred from experiencing the realization of self which comes from a skillful and devoted exercise of social duties. They would be deprived of one of the main forms of human good." We also posit a fundamental human need to affect one's social destiny that cannot be satisfied simply through economic affluence or exclusive preoccupation with private activity.

Finally we challenge the gloomy assessment itself. Without crediting the social system with perfect justice or claiming that it satisfies all citizens who press their case, there are countless examples of individuals and groups who have made an impact in public affairs. Nationally known people and organizations, within and outside of the electoral system, could be cited at length, but our purpose here is not to equate citizen action only with the style and commitment of Alinsky, King, Nader, Chisholm, Abzug, Goldwater, Rockefeller, or Buckley. Our concern is primarily with thousands of unnamed people working at the local to the international level, who may not attract the media's spotlight but who do make a difference on public issues. The Appendix lists a variety of activities undertaken by high school students trying to exert influence. Their successful projects include protecting recreational land from urban development, establishing youth service facilities (drug counseling center, home for runaways, black student union), preparing and advocating municipal plans, winning elections, and victorious legislative lobbying. Verba and Nie (1972), in a systematic study of adult participation, found that government leaders in a sample of communities were more responsive to active than to inactive citizens. That is, they were more aware of the activists' views, tended to share those views, and spent more of their efforts trying to implement them. Views of the inactive citizens were not as consistently known, shared, or pursued by government leaders. Powerful elites, the centralization of power, and the complexity of modern economic interdependence make citizen action difficult, even impossible in many situations. There is enough evidence, however, to indicate that the gloomy assessment is disputable and has not been conclusively demonstrated.[6]

Even if the extent to which the consent ideal can operate meaningfully is questionable, it should not be abandoned. Points raised in the gloomy assessment should instruct us not to view consent of the governed as an end state that at some point in time will or will not be achieved once and for all. Rather, it should communicate a sense of quest, a struggle toward an ideal recognized perhaps too often through our sense of its imperfect achievement, but worth pursuing nevertheless as a defining feature of our humanity. To forsake the principle on an uncertain suspicion that it may no longer be an appropriate foundation for the governance of public affairs would court the danger of inflicting upon ourselves a self-fulfilling prophecy.

Social Action: A Means

Discussion of our proposed curriculum may flounder by failing to note a distinction between the educational goal of increasing student ability to exert influence in public affairs and a pedagogical device used to achieve that goal, namely, student involvement in social action projects. We must further define social action and explain why it is a necessary, though not a sufficient nor an exclusive, component for curriculum aimed toward the objective of environmental competence in public affairs.

Social action might suggest only militant forms of public protest (marches, demonstrations, boycotts), but such is not our intent. It should be construed more generally to include any behavior directed toward exerting influence in public affairs. As such, it can include telephone conversations, letter writing, participation in meetings, research and study, testifying before public bodies, door-to-door can-

---

6. The fact that many citizens are apparently able to exert impact does not contradict our earlier summary of widespread lack of participation, knowledge, and efficacy in public affairs. To fulfill the consent ideal, this ability must be shared by not only a small proportion, but by all citizens.

vassing, fund-raising media production, bargaining and negotiation, and also publicly visible activity associated with the more militant forms. Social action can take place in or out of school and, if out of school, not necessarily in the streets, but in homes, offices, and workplaces. It might involve movement among several locations or concentration at one.

Student participation in such activities should not alone be considered evidence of social action. They might conduct a survey of attitudes toward the police only to assess the level of public support. They might distribute leaflets door to door, not to advocate a position, but to provide impartial information to help the citizenry make an informed decision. While these are examples of citizen participation from which much can be learned, they do not qualify as social action unless they are part of a strategy to affect public policy in a particular direction.

Types of issues can vary considerably. Students may wish to work for better bicycle trails, improved low-income housing, a "freer" school, opening of a drug counseling center, the election of a particular official. They might wish to oppose a curfew ordinance, high-rise apartments, credit practices of a particular firm, or a school's dress code. In pursuing such issues, students may be cast in the role of creative initiators or critical protestors. Most will be "followers"; some, "leaders."

This far-ranging conception should indicate the difficulty of claiming that all social action experience will guarantee students' gaining ability to exert influence in public affairs. We are all probably aware of activists who, in spite of high levels of participation, remain notoriously ineffective. They apparently learn very little through participation. An inspiring classroom lecture on the nature of representative government might conceivably give some students more help in exerting influence than participation in poorly executed community projects. We cannot, therefore, unconditionally endorse social action projects as the only vehicle for enhancing student ability to exert influence.

This qualification notwithstanding, social action experience is still absolutely necessary to increase ability to exert influence. Unfortunately, the argument for social action as a means to teach the exercise of influence is virtually circular, for the objective logically implies the means. It is similar to the problem we might have in explaining why students who wish to learn to swim should have an opportunity to go into the water. Learning to swim, by definition, requires "involvement" in water. Learning to exert influence in public affairs, by definition, requires involvement in attempts to influence public affairs, that is, in social action projects.

Social action projects can be the primary focus of laboratory experience which itself is but one component in a larger curriculum. The laboratory must be "well-equipped" with people in different roles (public officials, reporters, housewives, businessmen, laborers, parents, students), holding different views, and able to wield varying amounts of power on certain issues. It must have access to a variety of channels of communication such as mail, phone, radio, TV, printed media. Laboratory work will be done at a variety of sites: offices in public and private buildings, committee rooms, auditoriums, living rooms, sidewalks, parks, and schools. Curriculum materials must include legal documents, correspondence, books, magazines, films, research studies, budgets. The type of apparatus needed and the site of the work depend primarily upon the type of issue on which students attempt to exert influence, but it should be clear that social action projects generally require access to resources beyond the school building. Because social action projects might take students to a variety of places in a community, involve them with persons other than certified teachers, place them in the position of challenging the policies of existing regimes or adult authority, such student activity gives rise to a variety of reservations about citizen action curriculum.

Objections to Social Action Curriculum

Reservations about citizen action curriculum fall into two broad categories, not usually differentiated by critics. Some claim that it is impossible to achieve the goal of increasing student ability to exert influence in public affairs, while others are more concerned that, even if achievable, its pursuit will entail other harmful consequences.

Is the Objective Attainable?

The feasibility of the objective tends to be questioned on three grounds: teacher incompetence or unwillingness; lack of student readiness or interest; and community resistance.

Curriculum implications of this objective and one of its major means (social action experience) do imply significant departures from what usually occurs in schools. Teachers have not been educated to teach this type of curriculum; nor do the many adults in the community with whom students would work necessarily know how to help young people. Any attempt at implementing such a curriculum would have to encourage staff development, both within the school and with "community" teachers. Chapters 4 and 5 suggest some issues that such training might confront. At this early stage of development, however, problems of implementation can be postponed without jeopardizing the attempt to create a rationale for, and a general conception of, such a curriculum.

Another set of reservations is sensitive to the dynamics of human development. Adolescence has been characterized as a stage of life in which the individual's egocentric and interpersonal concerns take priority over concern for public affairs, where one is oriented to the immediate and the present rather than the future, where confusion, inconsistency, and unpredictability seem to prevail over ideology and clarity of commitment. Many adolescents may not have reached those higher stages in cognitive and moral development that facilitate effective participation. Because adolescents do not participate in the adult roles of bread winning, child rearing, and governing, they are also said to be ill prepared for decision making in public affairs. If this were a complete description of most adolescents, prospects for the effectiveness of citizen action curriculum would be dim indeed.

Developmental theory also suggests that, to avoid fixation at lower stages, persons need the challenge of problems that invite thought and behavior more complex or slightly "above" their current level of functioning. While careful research on this is yet to be done, observers of youth engaged in community involvement projects claim that their attempts to make a difference in the "real" world is precisely the kind of experience that facilitates cognitive and affective growth (Conrad, 1973). There is a danger that, by viewing developmental stages as inevitable and immutable, we create a self-fulfilling prophecy, for what children at various ages are "capable" of doing depends to some extent on what their culture asks of them (Ariés, 1962). While in America the acquisition of adult roles is for many children postponed for more than twenty years, recall that adolescents in days past operated businesses and ruled nations.[7]

Even today adolescence is described as a period when individuals begin to transcend egocentric orientations and gain the ability for sociocentric thinking (Adelson and O'Neil, 1966; Kohlberg, 1969). For many it is a time of profound social idealism. Some will speculate that adolescents might be more objective and fair-minded in their approach to public affairs precisely because they are not trapped by adult roles and vested power interests. Their apparent fickleness has also been construed as healthy flexibility, and the desire for role experimentation might be put to constructive purposes within citizen action efforts. Many adolescents have enough time for more intense and continuous participation than adults.

A judgment on whether adolescents are "capable" of effective participation also depends upon one's conception of those skills necessary for exerting influence. Influence can be exerted in a variety of ways that require differing levels of competence. As students work to develop personal styles of participation, some may find their strength in gathering information; others, in disseminating and publicizing; others, in public debate; others, in guiding group discussion; still others, in the competent performance of routine clerical work. To be effective as a citizen one need not, therefore, develop the host of talents characteristic of such "masters" of influence as a Lyndon Johnson or a Clarence Darrow. We must value a wide range of abilities or capabilities, any number of which can enhance a person's ability to make some impact on public matters.

On these grounds, we conclude that, whether adolescents are "capable" of effective participation in citizen action projects is at least problematic, and the possibility needs to be explored carefully through development and research. Even if we were to find that the majority of adolescents were "incapable," under the best possible educational program, of increasing their ability to exert influence,

---

7. Coleman (1972a), Panel on Youth (1974), and others argue that age segregation in our society is harmful to the socialization process. If adults and youth were to come together to work on common action goals, they would have more opportunity to communicate and examine the nature of adult-youth relations. Improved relations over the generation gap could, therefore, be a by-product of student involvement in social action. Although we do not wish to make the case for citizen action curriculum on these grounds, benefits such as these are conceivable, and should be examined more thoroughly.

one might still have an obligation to provide instruction for the small minority that could benefit.

Many point to community resistance as a major obstacle. Exerting influence may be a legitimate goal, but neither parents, businessmen, or government officials would support it, for it conjures up a variety of images contrary to normal expectations for schooling: too political, not focused on basic skills or preparation for careers or college, community disruption when unsupervised adolescents delve into public issues instead of sitting quietly in school "where they belong." Our proposal is undoubtedly different; perhaps it is "radical" enough to contradict conventional notions of schooling. A major aim of this book, however, is to present a sufficiently elaborate defense of the educational value of social action projects so that educators can respond to reservations that might otherwise lead to insurmountable community resistance. A full-fledged curriculum on exerting influence in public affairs requires considerable explanation and justification to taxpayers and others, but hundreds of educators and young people have already convinced their communities of the value of community involvement in secondary education. Across the nation there is mounting evidence that projects can anticipate sources of community opposition and deal with them constructively. Projects that have involved parents and community leaders in the conception and administration stages have experienced significant opposition only rarely.[8]

Are Other Results Harmful?

It is not enough to show that an educational program aims toward a valid objective and that the objective may be attainable. Suppose a program relies on pornographic novels to teach adolescents to increase reading speed and comprehension. The objective of improved

---

8. This is based on personal communication received from officials in organizations which promote and study youth participation projects throughout the country. Organizations contacted were the Center for Youth Development and Research, Minneapolis, Minn.; the Institute for Political-Legal Education, Pitman, N.J.; the National Association of Secondary School Principals, Reston, Va.; the National Commission on Resources for Youth, New York, N.Y. All the officials polled indicated that they were aware of no case in which community opposition was the primary reason for closing down a project. Only a small minority of the total projects on which information is available are involved in militant forms of citizen action. More information on each of these organizations is presented in the Appendix.

reading skills is widely accepted, and one might gather impressive evidence that the pornographic curriculum does in fact accomplish the objective. Yet the program might be rejected on the grounds that it violates community standards for appropriate literature. In addition to the educational needs of students, programs must also meet a vast array of community needs. These have been variously described as keeping young people off the labor market, providing employment for teachers, maintaining allegiance to the political-economic-legal system, holding the line on taxes, encouraging racial integration, or administering a nation-wide credentials system. Communities will vary in the extent to which they demand that all educational programs meet these criteria, but the educator must be able to face criticism based on such concerns.

The fact that curriculum must be defended not only on the basis of its benefit to individual students, but also on the basis of other criteria related to the community-at-large need not be viewed as a burden infringing on professional judgment. Though educators may disagree with particular demands that a given community makes, justification of a program with regard to community benefit is a legitimate professional responsibility. It should be construed not as a distasteful obligation to the commonweal, but as a positive opportunity to integrate concern for the development of individual students with concern for the needs of the larger community. In our attempt to justify the objective of increased ability to exert influence in public affairs, using social action as a means, we must anticipate other outcomes from the point of view of individual and community needs. Possible negative and positive consequences of citizen action curricula include:

Negative	Positive

Effects on individual students
1. Decreased ability to exert influence in public affairs.
2. Lack of knowledge or deficient background in the core subjects of general education: humanities, physical science, and social science.

1. Increased ability to exert influence.
2. Increased knowledge and improved background in humanities, physical science, and social science.

Exerting Influence in Public Affairs

3. Tendency to act impulsively rather than to study and reflect critically upon social problems.
4. Increased disillusionment with, and alienation from, the social system.

Effects on community

5. School becomes a tool for special political interests rather than a neutral resource for all people.
6. Increased destructive conflict and polarization in the community, and deterioration in the quality of public policy due to excessive participation of inexperienced youth.
7. Wasted resources on education since the curriculum will benefit only an extremely small proportion of the student body.

3. Tendency to base action more on reflection and study than on impulse.
4. Increased determination to "work within" or "on" the system rather than to drop out of it.

5. School becomes a more relevant neutral resource for all people, as it helps people become active.
6. Increase in constructive use of conflict, and improvement in public policy because of wider and better-educated citizen participation.

7. Well-invested resources in a large segment of the student body, or, if in a small segment, one that deserves it.

These possible consequences raise both the normative issue of deciding which consequences should be considered desirable or undesirable and the empirical one of predicting the probability of their occurrence. Although space does not permit extensive discussion of the normative problem and the empirical issue cannot really be settled without further development and research, the salience of these concerns in the minds of teachers, administrators, parents, and students compels us to deal with each point.

1. Our previous discussion of whether the objective can be accomplished is reflected here. For the sake of argument, we assume for the remainder of this section that the objective can be achieved and ask instead about the possibility of positive and negative side effects or by-products of pursuing that goal.

2. If students substitute citizen action curriculum for conventional courses in humanities and the physical and social sciences, they obviously will not acquire knowledge *as it is organized* in those courses. This is not to say, however, that they will acquire no knowledge in these fields. It will become apparent from the curriculum agenda in Chapter 3 that, in order to act effectively in public affairs, students need to master certain "content" and "methods of inquiry" generated in the disciplines. English, for example, is required for effective communication; physical science, for action on environmental issues; history and law, for action on constitutional rights; social science methods, for the study of attitudes or conditions in the community. Though specific knowledge gained in such areas may not conform identically to that offered in conventional courses, knowledge in the humanities, and the physical and social sciences can be acquired as a result of citizen action curriculum. Such a curriculum cannot be all things to all people, but, if it occupied only a portion of the student's secondary education, there would also be time for more conventional subjects.

3. Action may be perceived as inherently anti-intellectual in the sense that, once one decides to act, one in effect refuses to consider certain questions. For example, once you decide to work for passage of an equal rights amendment on the grounds that women are victims of widespread discrimination, your work does not encourage you to question whether there actually is widespread discrimination. Even if action does tend to define the limits within which inquiry occurs, this is no reason to characterize it as anti-intellectual, impulsive, or unreflective. To be effective, activists must inquire and reflect upon a variety of questions and, like scholars, they are expected to defend their conclusions to others.[9] These questions may involve complicated social research (What are the relative long-term costs of building new highways or developing mass transit to solve transportation needs?), ethical analysis (Is legalized abortion immoral?), or psychological introspection (Am I really trying to control people, rather than help them?). While social action may be undertaken impulsively and without sufficient study, the point of including it explicitly in

---

9. A defining characteristic of disciplined scholarship is the ability to restrict one's area of inquiry. Once a scientist begins an experiment, he or she, like the activist, is restrained from asking some questions in order that those under consideration can be thoroughly investigated. It would be inappropriate to describe this as anti-intellectual or impulsive behavior.

school curriculum is to remedy just this deficiency. If the curriculum is to help students exert influence effectively, it must increase, rather than decrease, reflective behavior.

4. Will student participation in social action tend to increase their commitment to democratic ideals or their faith in the existing political-economic system? Some fear that students, through involvement in public affairs, will be struck most of all by the shortcomings of institutions, will find dramatic disparity between ideals and reality, and will experience continual frustration in their attempts to affect society. The result could, therefore, be heightened disillusion, alienation, apathy, or revolt. Part of this prediction can be dismissed by recalling that at this point we are assuming a curriculum that increases student ability to exert influence in public affairs. The lack of ability to exert influence could not, therefore, be a source of disillusionment.

Still, we cannot deny the possibility that even persons capable of exerting influence and possessing a sense of efficacy might eventually choose to drop out or to take desperate revolutionary action. If these are conceivable consequences, they are risks we must take in order to find out whether society is seriously committed to widespread citizen action and whether the system can handle it. To deny students the opportunity to exert influence in public affairs on the grounds that it would reduce their commitment to democracy (both the ideal and the particular system that claims to have implemented the ideal) would be a ludicrous contradiction. This risk is of little concern to me, for I predict that most persons who gain increased ability to exert influence will feel better able to cope with the system and less inclined toward either withdrawal or revolution.[10]

5. For those who view school as a neutral, impartial citadel of wisdom standing above the biases and passions of political-economic life, the prospect of school-sponsored student involvement in public

---

10. Schwartz (1973) offers evidence that political alienation is not associated with any single approach to political participation. Though persons involved in politics are often "alienated," alienated people exhibit a wide range of behavior: conformity, reformism, ritualism, retreatism, rebelliousness. According to Schwartz, the adoption of any of these seems to be a function of the extent to which the person under consideration (*a*) perceives conflict between his values and those of the system; (*b*) feels *personally* ineffective; (*c*) perceives the *system* as ineffective (i.e., not responding to legitimate grievances); and (*d*) values participation. If all these conditions are present, active involvement still occurs, and Schwartz calls this "alienated reformism."

affairs can be frightening, indeed. The fear is that groups with special political interests will begin to dominate the curriculum, thereby violating the professional integrity which, presumably, educators alone bring to subject matter. If commitment to social causes were to replace dispassionate inquiry as a goal of education, would we not risk infringement on academic freedom and freedom of speech? A response to this point depends upon one's conception of the alleged "political neutrality" of state-supported schools.

Let us accept the proposition that, in a certain sense, the school ought to be as "politically neutral" as possible. That is, it should be a model of pluralism in which students are free to learn about a variety of political philosophies and cultural styles. Inquiry should not be restricted by the temporary objectives of specific political, economic, or ethnic groups. The academic justification for this notion of neutrality is that "truth" itself cannot be ascertained without uncensored investigation of a wide range of alternative "answers" to the important "questions" of life. There is also a political justification for academic freedom. The consent ideal requires the state to ensure that all groups have a reasonably equal chance to express themselves in order that they have a reasonably equal chance to govern themselves. In this sense the insistence on political neutrality in specific matters stems from a more general political vision, and the school cannot, therefore, be neutral with regard to the consent ideal. As a vehicle of the state, the school must work to fulfill this political principle and can be considered "politically neutral" only in a limited sense.

Thus, for both academic and political reasons the school should design programs that cultivate in every student the ability to exert influence, whether one holds a minority or a majority point of view, whether one belongs to a group that has negligible or awesome power. Student action projects should be able to confront and oppose each other. Some may work for increases in welfare payments; others, for decreases. Some may lobby for more parks; others, for more parking lots. Opposing candidates might each have students working in their organizations. To the extent that a school is committed to pluralism of this sort, it can stimulate free inquiry, which could keep it from becoming a "tool" of special interests. In this sense it remains "neutral," even when its students can be politically active.

A school might encourage action projects considered "constructive" (for example, volunteer programs for the elderly), but prohibit others (for example, a campaign to expose financial investments of school officials). To the extent that projects become censored, not for moral or legal reasons, but to maintain the power of a particular regime, the school is no longer neutral. It is possible to conclude that schools never have been or even can be neutral, for their very existence depends upon the political and economic support of constituencies with specific biases. Where this interpretation prevails, citizen action projects may help students exert influence in public affairs, but only in narrow directions acceptable to the establishment. To the extent that schools restrict the range of action that students may undertake, they no doubt violate the pluralistic philosophy we advocate. We must recognize, however, that indoctrination, partisanship, or one-sidedness arising from group attempts to maintain power are problems that pervade all curricula; they are not unique to citizen action. If we conclude that schools by their nature are inevitably and exclusively involved in power maintenance, then the question is not whether schools should support student action projects, but whether schools will tolerate *any* learning that might pose a threat to the values and policies of existing regimes. It is possible, of course, that many schools will sincerely endorse the neutrality and pluralism advocated here, if only because such openness would increase student support for school authorities.

6. Heightened student ability to exert influence in public affairs conveys to some a specter of increased conflict, polarization, deterioration of policy, and even a breakdown in the governing system itself. This concern usually emerges from a prediction that hordes of unenlightened activists will descend upon public officials so continuously and persistently that the day-to-day functions of government would be crippled and no stable long-term policy could be implemented.

To be sure, persons who feel politically efficacious (and let us assume their sense of efficacy signifies the actual ability to make an impact) participate more frequently in public than those who do not (Almond and Verba, 1963; Robinson *et al.*, 1968). Yet even those who feel efficacious are not involved continuously; participation among even the able is likely to be selective and episodic. People function in many roles, only one of which is "citizen," and the countless activities of human interest beyond so-called acts of citizenship leave little time for involvement in public affairs. The process of exerting influence is unlikely to bring immediate rewards and certainly not personal material benefits or increased social approval. Though definite psychological satisfactions can come from active participation and from goal achievement, the work is not always pleasant; often there is stress and conflict. Finally, continuous massive citizen participation on all issues can work against one's interest. To be effective, one should not spread efforts too widely. Participation should concentrate on those few issues or campaigns that seem most significant, and the collective power of groups, rather than frenetic actions of isolated individuals, should be used. It is fully acknowledged by intelligent activists that the successful exercise of influence itself requires restraints on participation. For these reasons we should not predict levels of participation escalating to a point that overloads the very consent system that attempts to preserve the right of participation itself. Even Almond and Verba (1963), who decry continuous massive citizen participation, agree that all citizens must have ability to exert influence, be it used only occasionally. Unless elites believe that all citizens have the potential for high levels of participation, those who govern will respond only to the interests of special groups. To the extent that individuals and groups vary in their ability to influence the elite, we fall short of the consent ideal.

Some might see citizen action curriculum as fostering increased student awareness of the complexity of the system, yielding more citizen patience and less "noise" in public affairs. Those students who become highly involved may choose issues of only limited interest to the community-at-large (forming a black student union, expanded counseling service for runaways, organizing a student cooperative). Some students might engage in action projects aimed precisely at *reducing* conflict and polarization through publicly sponsored rap groups, lectures, TV programs, or attitude surveys. Conflict on some matters might increase, and that on others might decrease as a result of social action curriculum.

Finally, one might question the notion of conflict as undesirable. Cognitive conflict has been shown to enhance intellectual growth; interpersonal conflict within training groups has been shown to have beneficial therapeutic effects; conflict has even been described as a

Exerting Influence in Public Affairs

"healthy organizational process," stimulating diagnosis, communication, group cohesiveness, improved communication, and leadership (Chesler et al., 1972). Increased ability to exert influence in public affairs could well involve an orientation not to end conflict categorically, but to use and manage it toward desirable ends.

One root of the concern for conflict is a fear that students in social action projects will expose themselves to risks of personal injury, both physical and psychological. Will they be beaten, gassed, arrested, verbally abused, publicized, given a record or a reputation that will haunt them for the rest of their lives? The conception of citizen action curriculum proposed here does not entail such risks. First, it has been explained that militant, publicly visible forms of protest constitute only one of many types of social action. Second, the point of developing a curriculum for social action is to help students evaluate more systematically the way in which they wish to participate. Those initially inclined toward riskier forms of action should be encouraged to examine the risks carefully. If students happen to choose a course of action which a teacher cannot condone, such as illegal acts of civil disobedience, the teacher must make students aware of the risks, indicate that the school in no way supports or sponsors such activity, and, with the students' knowledge, inform parents of the school's position. On the basis of past experience, this is unlikely to arise, but, if students are threatened with personal injury, teachers and school officials have a clear obligation, legally and morally, to protect them. Participation in disputes on public affairs does not, however, appreciably increase the possibility of such injury;[11] therefore, the obligation to look out for the students' welfare does not require that they be insulated from participation on community issues.

What about the charge that, because of the inability of lay citizens, especially youth, to comprehend substantive complexities in public affairs (dynamics of thermal pollution or the economics of oil production), increased participation leads to the adoption of less intelligent policies? In a sense the charge cannot be either verified or refuted. For many issues, it is impossible to make an impartial, objective assessment of the wisdom, rationality, intelligence, or propriety of public actions—the most knowledgeable experts disagree on the

---

11. Chapter 4 contains a more detailed discussion of liability.

"right" solution. Even if we could make reliable judgments about the quality of certain policies, do we have any consistent historical evidence that low citizen participation has resulted in the adoption of better policies than high participation? There are notable examples of disasters perpetrated when there were low levels of citizen involvement (the Bay of Pigs invasion, the initial commitment of U.S. troops to Vietnam). Intelligent participators are likely to recognize issues which, because of their complexity, should not be decided by the layman, but properly delegated to more knowledgeable authorities. Finally, and perhaps most important, there is the major premise in the consent principle itself, namely, that the people might well make mistakes but the right to govern themselves includes the right to make their own mistakes, and this political principle is more fundamental than the hope that the decisions judged "right" by some hypothetical, disinterested observer will be made.

The concern that youth present special problems for the consent ideal is legitimate, and were we to argue that all persons above the age of five be given the full rights of adult citizenship, the prediction that policy deterioration would occur might seem more plausible. Since we limit our proposal to adolescents and even then do not advocate their having unilateral control on any issue, possible dangers diminish. Because adults hold most of the power on most issues, youth will have to learn how to deal with them. If adults, in their "more mature wisdom," require particular types of arguments, evidence, and approaches, then youth, to exert influence, will have to conform to many of the same standards.

Suppose, for the sake of argument, that youth did gain enough political, legal, and economic power to control a community. Some profess that, under the influence of youth, public policy would not suffer, but improve: their "innocence"—that is, lack of vested interests, axes to grind, power to maintain—would enable them to study more objectively than adults what is needed for the general welfare. Though we need not accept this, we can suggest that variance in intelligence, ability to govern, and sense of values among youth is probably as great as it is among adults. Youth are, perhaps, equally "qualified" to govern in the sense that they may make the same kinds of mistakes as adults. The effect of youth participation on public policy is probably impossible to determine, but the objective of increasing student ability to exert influence is not put forth on the grounds that it will bring more wisdom or rationality to specific public policies.

7. Some may oppose citizen action curriculum on the claim that only a small proportion, say 5 percent, of the students would be interested enough to benefit. To devote substantial resources to such a small minority would be wasteful, unjustly depriving the student majority of instruction more in keeping with their interests. This estimate of student interest seems accurate only because of a conception of social action far more restrictive than the one presented here. Recall that our conception of citizen participation is not oriented toward the full-time crusader or leader of conspicuous national movements. There should be ample opportunity within the curriculum to work on the "big" issues and to identify with a Ralph Nader, a Shirley Chisholm, or a William Buckley, but we cannot lose sight of local groups supporting issues that are not widely publicized but that relate, nevertheless, to public affairs most significant in the lives of the "typical" citizen. Examples include a local organization for the mentally retarded that wants to influence school curriculum to be more responsive to its constituency; a local chapter of the Urban League that wants a summer recreation program to put more resources into ghetto playgrounds; a local motorcycle club that needs permission to hold races on vacant public land; a church's social action committee that wants youth appointed to municipal boards; an Audubon club that wants to protect natural areas from highway expansion; a theater group that seeks a public subsidy. Most communities have dozens of such volunteer organizations that often take action in the public realm. While many such organizations are dominated by adults, young people do participate. Young people also have their own organizations. When a conception of citizen action is broadened to include such activities, the estimated percentage of potentially interested students increases considerably, perhaps to a majority.

Yet, even when citizen action curriculum is viewed more narrowly as attracting only the relatively few people interested in the genre of activism reported in the media, there is justification for expenditure of school resources.[12] If majority interest were a criterion for all

12. It has been suggested that a curriculum aimed at skills in the exercise of influence would tend to serve liberals, radicals, or revolutionaries, but not conservatives, for conservatives are assumed to be satisfied with the world as it is, or at least to wish less intervention through governmental auspices. Verba and Nie (1972) find, however, the most active segment of the population to be white, upper-status, wealthy, middle-aged citizens who take relatively conservative positions at least on welfare issues. Persons who wish to curb governmental power and persons who wish existing policies to remain untouched often exert influ-

educational offerings, schools would probably have to abolish instruction in many areas, from French to physics. In fact, if all subjects were voluntary, perhaps no single course could attract a majority of students. To the extent that any minority of students ought to have its educational interests met, the activists deserve part of the pie. It can be argued, furthermore, that investing educational resources in a minority of serious activists will benefit the public at large. If they are educated to be more responsible, judicious, and efficient in their work, perhaps fewer resources might ultimately be wasted on unnecessary controversy or ineffective attempts at influence. While the argument for citizen action curriculum cannot stand on this point alone, it does suggest that spending educational resources on a "minority" might bring public benefits.

It is clear, from considering seven possible reservations concerning a citizen action curriculum, that each "negative" has a conceivable "positive" counterpart. Furthermore, the actual consequences of social action curriculum will depend more upon the idiosyncratic way in which it is implemented in a community than on the generally conceived objective and means presented here. One educator might promise to design a curriculum in such a way as to ensure achievement of only the "positive" goals. Another will claim that implementation cannot be controlled sufficiently to ensure these goals and that lack of control will inevitably lead to negative ones. A third might reply that lack of control over specific types of student involvement does not necessarily result in either positive or negative consequences. Given our definitions of "ability to exert influence in public affairs" and "social action," anticipation of negative consequences is not logically warranted. More conclusive findings on actual outcomes of citizen action curriculum growing out of this model must await empirical investigation.

The "Hidden" Social Philosophy

Readers will reasonably search for important assumptions in this position that may not yet have been mentioned. Is Newmann a Jeffersonian, a pluralist, a rationalist, a capitalist, a social reconstruc-

---

ence to protect their interests. The felt need for actively exerting influence probably depends less upon one's general ideological orientation and more upon whether one's interests happen to be served by those in power in a given situation.

tionist? What ultimate social vision is implied by this interpretation of the consent principle, and what is the role of public education in fulfilling it? Without trying to justify every assumption that may lie at the heart of the position, I can identify some which speak to such questions.

As a human who, of necessity, makes normative choices, my ultimate value commitment is the general notion of human dignity which rests upon the more specific values of equality, freedom of choice, and rationality. These are discussed, along with a rejection of ethical relativism, in Newmann and Oliver (1970). For further support of these value judgments, I rely on the work of Kohlberg (1971) and Rawls (1971).

From a perspective, not as an educator, but as a social critic, I conclude that, to achieve such values, a society first needs to provide for procedures or institutional mechanisms of decision making that seem to lead to realization of the values. This emphasis on process should be distinguished from prescriptions for substantive policy. One might argue, for example, that the best way to achieve human dignity is to distribute the wealth equally, or to conserve energy by banning the automobile. Unfortunately, a great variety of substantive policies, some of them contradictory, can often be defended with regard to these general values and, furthermore, our view of the "correct" policies is likely to change significantly through time. Thus, it is not fruitful to seek the attainment of basic values exclusively through proposals for substantive policy. The structure and distribution of power and the institutionalized procedures that generate those policies are more fundamental. For reasons already presented, the ideal of consent of the governed is the most appropriate procedural principle for the achievement of these values, although, as indicated, this ideal is far from realization (see Myrdal, 1974) in the United States.

The social "vision" implied by this position is no more specifically drawn than whatever is connoted by a flourishing consent system in which each citizen has access to public decisions and the ability to exert influence according to one's intentions. I have deliberately tried to avoid sketching many details in this vision. One might ask, for example, whether, in order to have such a consent system, the society should abolish private property, break up corporate bureaucracy, transfer political and economic power to neighborhood groups, limit geographic and social mobility, or abandon standardized credentials and the idea of a meritocracy. Though I support several specific efforts to "open up the system" (for example, "affirmative action," power structure research, Naderism, Common Cause), there are many issues which, in my view, have not been sufficiently analyzed to produce a set of substantive policies that could be confidently adopted as a complete picture of the ideal consent system. With this degree of uncertainty, it would be inappropriate to infer from my position the existence of a specifically drawn societal blueprint.[13]

Given the goal of an active consent system as a necessary route to human dignity, the educator could develop curricula intended to convince students to support and work for specific policies which, in the educator's judgment, would be required to strengthen the consent system, or one could increase student ability to exert influence according to whatever substantive policy they, as autonomous social critics, decided to pursue (assuming, of course, that such goals would not violate the consent ideal). The first of these strategies is educationally indefensible for three reasons. It is often unclear which particular policies ought to be sought. In denying students the opportunity to inquire openly about the causes they wish to support, the curriculum would also fail to teach independent inquiry on policy questions, a competence required for maintenance of the consent ideal. Finally, advocating specific policy as the core of curriculum for all students would violate the principle of school neutrality. The second strategy is more defensible on the grounds that it is more intellectually responsible, allows for development of autonomous student inquiry, and does not violate the principle of school neutrality on specific policy.

Ability to Exert Influence and Other Goals in Secondary Curriculum

Until now environmental competence in public affairs has been considered the single important objective for all students in second-

---

13. The vision does include a series of constitutional rights implied by the consent ideal: universal suffrage; rights to free speech, assembly, petition, recall, referenda; access to public meetings and information; majority rule; periodic elections for relatively short terms of office, etc.

ary education. There are, of course, many other worthwhile things for people to learn and a multitude of demands on schools to teach them. Schools are urged to help people engage in productive work (career education); in satisfying leisure (arts, athletics); in meaningful interpersonal relations (communication skills, intergroup relations, marriage and family). They have been asked to help students protect their personal health and safety and their financial security (consumer education). In relation to these various goals, what priority should be given to effective citizenship, and what part of the curriculum should be devoted to its pursuit?

It should be clear from the argument thus far that the ability to exert influence is construed as general education, that is, an objective appropriate for all students.[14] Many of the above goals might also be put forth as aspects of general education. Assuming that public schools cannot, indeed, should not, be all things to all people, and that, however difficult the choices, priorities must be established, we dare to suggest that ability to exert influence in public affairs be considered the top priority for general education. This objective cannot, and should not, be handled by social studies alone. Many aspects of the curriculum should be directed toward it.

This position finds support in two lines of reasoning. First, we must realize that many of the other goals proposed for the secondary curriculum could not be achieved except in a political democracy with a healthy consent system. To make intelligent choices about the vocational skills one wants to learn requires a political-economic system that provides for individual vocational choice. To appreciate great works of literature, art, or music requires a system that allows for open expression of these interests. To explore alternative forms of interpersonal relations requires a system that permits a diversity of life styles. To become an intelligent consumer or "decision maker" requires a system with wide public access to information. Many of these educational goals reflect valued components of "the good life"

---

14. Chapters 1 and 2 have tried only to establish the educational goal. Chapter 4 explains why actual coursework in the exercise of influence should not, at this point, be required of all students, but should be available for all to elect on a voluntary basis. There is an important distinction between increasing ability to exert influence in public affairs as a goal valid for all versus a program requirement (i.e., a restriction on freedom) which, in embryonic stages of curriculum development, could offer no assurance that students' competence would in fact be enhanced.

or "the pursuit of happiness" in a democracy, and, without a democratic consent system, many of these very goals would be inconceivable or possibly illegitimate. (Imagine, for example, goals for public education in a totalitarian society.) In this sense, the maintenance and enhancement of the democratic consent system is fundamentally important to education. To the extent that the school neglects its mission in strengthening that system, it will, in the long run, undermine efforts to fulfill these other legitimate educational aims.

Second, given scarce resources and the inability of a single institution to achieve all conceivable worthwhile forms of education, we must ask whether the public secondary school, compared with other institutions, might be more suited to accomplish some objectives, while nonschool institutions might more appropriately teach others. Newmann and Oliver (1967) offer suggestions for restricting the jurisdiction of school, and Coleman (1972a) suggests that, of eight basic competencies required in socialization from child to adult, the school is appropriately equipped to provide only one. To involve youth directly with adults at their workplaces may be a more effective route to vocational or career education. To offer more support for nonschool youth organizations may be a more effective strategy for teaching interpersonal and intergroup relations. Making greater use of museums and of dramatic and musical productions in the nonschool world may more adequately provide for education in these areas. The family, in spite of many obituaries announcing its death, continues to provide a remarkably effective learning environment where skills in homemaking, child care, counseling, and even reading are mastered. It is conceivable that many reasonable educational aims now pursued by secondary schools could be "delegated" to other institutions.

Unfortunately, however, there seems to be no appropriate substitute institution for teaching about the consent system and how to exert influence within it. One might assign this task to "the government," and send children off to learn in the offices of legislators, lobbyists, journalists, or attorneys. Such apprenticeships could be valuable, even required, for parts of the curriculum, but it would be unwise to entrust any political body or interest group with the obligation of educating all students for the effective exercise of influence. Because political regimes, parties, and interest groups function in an almost exclusively partisan role, they cannot be committed to the broad view of citizen participation advocated here. One could not expect an organization to teach directions or styles of influence that might jeopardize the interests of the very partisan organization sponsoring the curriculum.

Though the school will depend upon students' experience in partisan contexts, it, alone among institutions, seems potentially capable of maintaining the detachment implied in the commitment to help every student learn to exert influence as he or she sees fit. We grant that a school can have vested interests in particular political decisions (for example, bond issues and budgets). With these exceptions, it can, nevertheless, remain theoretically committed to help each student increase ability to exert influence without contradicting or impeding its official function to preserve and enhance the consent system. The school, then, in spite of all its faults, continues to offer a critically needed structure for the pursuit of citizenship education.

We have argued for the salience of environmental competence in public affairs in a constellation of other possible general education goals for the secondary school. As we proceed to develop an agenda for the kinds of competencies (knowledge, skills, and attitudes) required by such a goal, it should become clear that our curriculum is likely to produce spin-offs or by-products that fulfill other goals as well. As was indicated earlier, communication skills are critical for the effective exercise of influence, and substantive knowledge in the sciences and social sciences is likely to result from such a curriculum. Involvement in public issues can increase one's knowledge in areas that range from consumerism to the arts. The choice of ability to exert influence as a top curriculum priority in no way precludes the achievement of other objectives. Advocating it as top priority is only to indicate that, in case of a conflict between objectives, often manifested through competing demands for resources or for students' time, environmental competence in public affairs should not be sacrificed or become subordinate to other objectives.

CHAPTER 3
An Agenda for Curriculum Development

If increasing student ability to exert influence in public affairs is accepted as a valid educational objective, what kinds of knowledge, skills, attitudes, attributes, or competencies are associated with such ability? Once the general objective is broken down into specific components, one might then be able to design a curriculum appropriate for each.[1] The purpose here is to outline topics or areas of competence to serve as a focus for future development of instructional materials, teaching strategies, approaches to student advising and counseling, and program structures. The model is not deliberately derived from any particular theory of human behavior, social structure, or political process, but from my general synthesis of literature in social science, education, and social activism and from my personal experience in curriculum development, teaching, and citizen action.

Summary of the Model

In an elaboration of the model presented earlier, in Figure 1, the major components that a citizen action curriculum needs to teach can be found in Figure 2. Prior to exerting influence or trying to implement a position, a person should clarify and justify particular policies, candidates, and actions that he or she supports or opposes. These become one's goals or desired outcomes in public affairs. They

---

1. Limitations of this approach to curriculum design are discussed at the end of this chapter.

Agenda for Curriculum Development

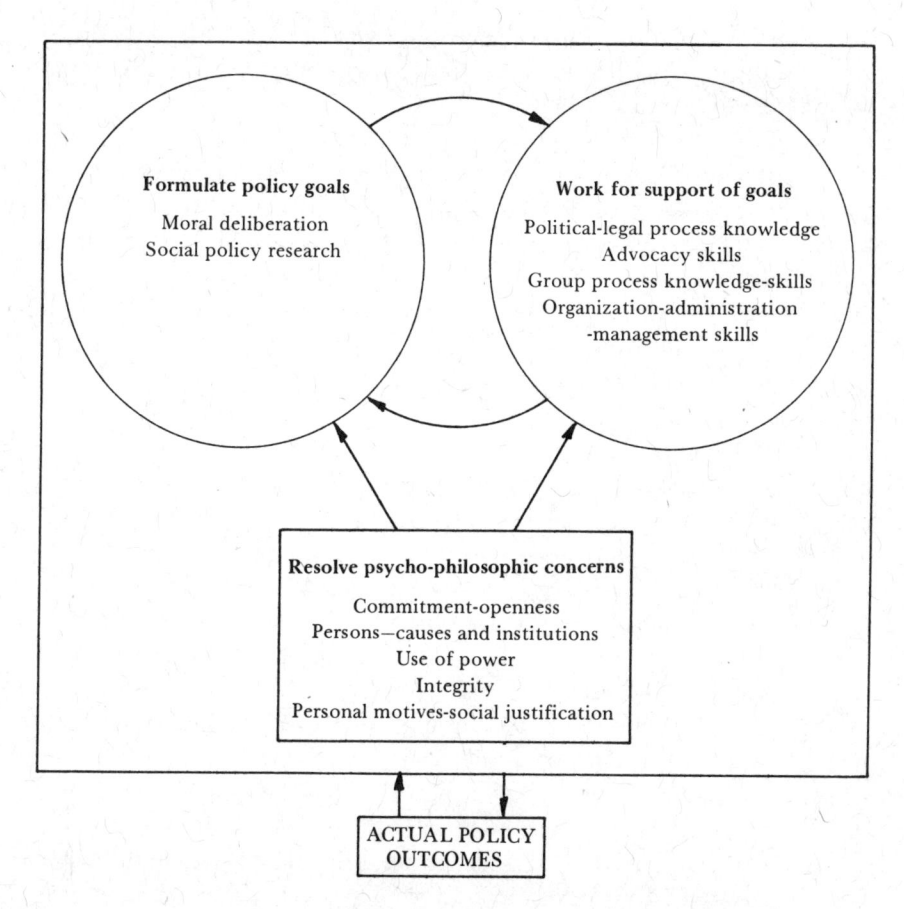

FIGURE 2
Areas of competence required to exert influence in public affairs

should be formulated not on the basis of impulse, whim, or duress, but upon principled moral deliberation and responsible social research. That is, prescriptive claims involving possible value conflicts ("We ought to legalize abortion."), should be justified through a principled, ethical framework, and controversial empirical, definitional, or legal claims ("The parents of unwanted children and the children themselves lead a life of suffering.") should be supported with as much evidence as possible.

Having formulated goals (for example, repeal of an antiabortion law, starting an abortion counseling service, or electing an official who would press on these matters), the citizen works to muster support after determining whose support is required to implement the goal. Accurate information is required on both how power is distributed and how decisions are made within institutions relevant to the goal, which can be summarized as knowledge of the realities of political-legal process. To communicate and justify the goal to appropriate individuals, agencies, or publics, advocacy skills in writing, speaking, and the use of various media are needed. Assistance from different groups, also critical in mobilizing support, makes knowledge of group behavior and skills in group dynamics a third component. Finally, effective campaign management requires record keeping, planning, and scheduling of meetings, fund raising, negotiation tactics, and other practical competencies summarized as skills in organization-administration-management.

In formulating goals and in trying to win support, a number of concerns, which we label "psycho-philosophic dilemmas," are likely to confront the activist. Suppose one person is so ambivalent that he cannot act with conviction on any public issue, or another feels so omnipotent that she often sets goals impossible to achieve. Some citizens may be reluctant to act because they see public controversy mainly as a form of interpersonal warfare, and they shy away from "hurting people." Others may have difficulty trying to decide how much they can compromise without losing their personal integrity. Some may participate, but they experience feelings of guilt when personal motives for acting do not seem to match the ostensible social justification of the cause. Because the stress and anxiety roused by these concerns may interfere with productive action, a citizen action curriculum should attempt to help people resolve such matters in ways that allow for more effective exercise of influence.

The model may, at this point, seem overly idealized or formalized. Certainly all the activities of effective citizens cannot be neatly charted according to these components. Nor should the components be viewed as being isolated from one another or as being organized in linear sequence. The process of winning support may actually assist in clarifying goals. Involvement in advocacy and persuasion may lead to deeper moral deliberation or further policy research. Psycho-philosophic concerns may either encourage certain action strategies or result from them. In other words, the parts of the model continually interact in patterns that are idiosyncratic to the nature of each person's involvement in a given issue. The components were outlined here in order to focus attention on specific and theoretically distinct aspects in the general conception of an ability to exert influence in public affairs. Analytic dissection makes it easier to see whether or how well the existing curriculum covers various facets involved in the exercise of influence. The secondary curriculum may already deal with some of the components indirectly, but the model offers a totally new agenda for instruction.

Formulating Policy Goals

Moral Deliberation

Recommendations that a particular public policy be adopted, that a candidate be elected, or that an agency take a specific action are often based on prescriptive or normative claims. Justifying such recommendations may be difficult, for at times people are committed to apparently conflicting value claims. The principle of freedom of the press, for example, seems to preclude restrictions on the reporting of criminal prosecutions and trials. The principle of due process or fair trial, on the other hand, seems to require such restrictions in order to avoid bias in legal proceedings. A landlord committed to property rights may oppose an equal opportunity ordinance that limits his ability to select tenants, but a prospective tenant may insist that discrimination in selection of tenants be outlawed on the grounds that equal opportunity should take priority over property rights. Many value conflicts involve disputes about the rights and obligations of individuals and individual interests as opposed to those of a larger community. Articulating and justifying the normative principles behind one's recommendations in public affairs is, in this sense, a form of moral deliberation.

It has been argued that normative claims or expressions of preference in public affairs are subjective choices that cannot be proved either true or false or morally right or wrong in any reliable, objective, or universally acceptable way. Each person, according to this view, is entitled to hold any position on questions of values. When values concerning public affairs conflict, some people feel that the question of which value ought to prevail cannot be solved "rationally" through ethical reasoning, but only through the harsh realities of political-economic struggle. However, Veatch (1962), Newmann and Oliver (1970), and Kohlberg and Mayer (1972) show why this position of subjective relativism must be rejected. Jurisprudential and ethical theorists have demonstrated that distinctions can be made between more and less adequate ways of justifying value preferences and that standards can and should be universally applied to value claims put forth in support of public policy.

The standards include criteria for the *process of argument* as well as for the *substantive values* on which the arguments are grounded. In the realm of process, for example, one should be able to justify a decision on specific cases by reference to general value claims. One should be able to test the consistency of one's commitment to general value claims by examining real and hypothetical cases that are analogous but might involve potentially conflicting values. As apparent inconsistencies or contradictions in one's value preferences arise, a person should be able to resolve them by articulating some hierarchy of values, or by noticing distinctions or arriving at definitions that resolve alleged logical conflicts. Finally, one is obligated to engage in rational process, giving reasons for preferences on public matters and seriously answering challenges to this reasoning. Oliver and Shaver (1974) and Newmann and Oliver (1970) have further elaborated this process of moral deliberation as it applies to public policy issues.

In the realm of substantive values, moral deliberation requires a rejection of ethical relativism and an acceptance of equal respect for the life of each human being as the ultimate, universally appropriate value. Such a value orientation holds, for example, that the right to life generally takes precedence over the right to control one's property, that laws can be unjust and immoral when they violate the highest moral principle, that one is not entitled to pursue individual self-interest to the point where it violates equal respect for another's life. Kohlberg's discussion of postconventional moral reasoning (1971) and Newmann and Oliver's discussion of the value of individual dignity (1970) offer further explanation of primary values that should serve as the basis of moral deliberation.

Lockwood (1970) has explored the possibility that adherence to postconventional principles of justice, as outlined by Kohlberg, is at least a correlate, if not a prerequisite, of the sophisticated cognitive operations demanded in the curriculum of Newmann, Oliver, and

Shaver. If the use of such principles and cognitive processes is a function of naturally occurring developmental stages, as the works of Kohlberg (1969, 1971) and Piaget (1937) suggest, then there may be limits on the extent to which moral deliberation can be taught. Some persons may be capable of attaining the highest stages of reasoning only at certain ages; others, never. However, there has been no significant attempt to experiment with curriculum in order to determine the extent to which stages of reasoning can be elevated through instruction. Thus, we must not discriminate between persons "educable" and "noneducable" in these matters, lest it become a self-fulfilling prophecy.

There are two main reasons why we should attempt to teach an approach to moral deliberation guided by process and substantive values. As argued earlier, no person should be given a blank check to exercise his will in public affairs; each citizen has a moral duty to justify the policies and values advocated if they affect the lives of others. And, from a pragmatic point of view, those who do master the skills of jurisprudential argument and who do reason on the basis of the "higher" values will be able to exert more influence than those who do not. Because such individuals would be able to deal with arguments or justifications at all levels of moral reasoning, they would have the potential, all other things being equal, of being far more persuasive than persons with less developed abilities in these areas.[2]

Discussion of universal standards of morality or of "higher" levels of moral reasoning carries elitist and imperialistic implications that may offend those committed to egalitarian and pluralistic ideals. Realizing this, it is important to explain why the proposal made here does not necessarily pose such threats. First, the ultimate commitment to equal respect for each individual life implies both equality and diversity, not elitism or imperialism. Jurisprudential analytic operations are meant to serve this ultimate value. What is more important, however, is that there is a critical limitation (or strength, depending upon one's view) in the theoretical power of the Newmann and Oliver (1970), Oliver and Shaver (1974), and Kohlberg

---

2. Research has shown that persons at a given stage of development are impressed by arguments one (or sometimes two) levels above their own. Thus, persons operating at the higher levels of reasoning can more easily influence persons at a lower level than vice versa (Rest, Turiel, and Kohlberg, 1969).

(1969, 1971) works. None of the frameworks argue—on the contrary, they clearly deny—that universal use of jurisprudential analytic operations would provide unequivocal answers to all controversies arising from different value preferences.

Even if jurisprudential process and commitment to the "higher" values could be successfully taught to all citizens, there would still be lack of consensus on much public policy. Persons operating at the highest stages of cognitive and moral development often disagree because there is uncertainty regarding factual claims, an uncertainty originating not in different value commitments but in deficiencies in knowledge about the effects of human action. Neither the physical nor the social sciences have been able to produce indisputable answers to many questions of public importance: What fiscal policies are most likely to control inflation in certain situations? What is the effect of interracial bussing on school achievement? What effect will income maintenance plans have on employment, crime, or one's sense of self-worth? Is a particular product harmful to health? Legitimate controversy also abounds among "sophisticated" thinkers on definitions or questions of meaning: At what point is a fetus a "human being" and thereby entitled to "rights"? What physiological signs should be recognized as equivalent to "death"? What are "high crimes and misdemeanors"? What is a "clear and present danger" to the state or community? This inevitable indeterminacy with regard to many empirical and definitional issues accounts for the fact that even Kohlberg's theory recognizes that different policy conclusions can emerge from any two people operating at the same stage, including the highest, in moral development.[3]

Our recommendations for procedural and substantive values to guide moral deliberation do not rest, therefore, on the belief that, through their use, truth in public affairs would be universally apparent or that ethical disagreement would cease. Our claim is that these frameworks, if successfully taught, would resolve rationally and in

---

3. Warnock's (1967) explanation of indeterminacy in moral reasoning mentions lack of information about the future course of events, lack of consensus on the meaning of the "welfare" of human beings, the need to weigh short-term good and harm against long-term good and harm, the need to weigh good and harm to some individuals against good and harm to others, and the need to weigh good and harm accruing to a single individual. For these reasons, he claims it is "extremely uncommon ... for moral reasoning to lead indisputably to just one particular conclusion" (p. 70).

ethically acceptable form a number of controversies that could not otherwise be resolved; and the universal use of these frameworks, if used to examine the multitude of issues remaining unresolved, would produce debate and dialogue more acceptable from an ethical and epistemological point of view. In conclusion, it must be emphasized that students who do master the frameworks are in no sense more entitled to participate in public affairs than those who do not. While those competent in sophisticated moral deliberation may be potentially more influential and persuasive, to deny the less competent the right to social participation would violate the very principle of equality that justifies the moral framework itself.

Social Policy Research

How should we handle disputes in public affairs that do not arise solely as a result of conflicting value preferences but from disagreement over descriptive or factual claims about the actual effects of policies in the past, present, or future? In the Vietnam conflict, both hawks and doves claimed ultimate allegiance to the value of peace, but they disagreed as to which policy (military escalation or withdrawal) was more likely to achieve that value. Opponents of guaranteed minimum income may claim that it will lead to decreased productivity and indolence, but proponents challenge that claim. Students concerned with equal rights may have difficulty determining the extent to which discrimination based on race or sex actually occurs. The long-term costs and benefits of such policies as abortion on demand, legalization of marijuana, shelter homes for runaway youth, and bussing to achieve racial balance raise empirical questions that can generate as much heat and can be as difficult to resolve as controversies rooted more directly in value conflicts.

Definitional controversies have similar significance. Should the Vietnam conflict be characterized as civil war or foreign aggression? What is an unreasonable search? What constitutes equal educational opportunity? Establishing criteria for key concepts and determining whether a particular set of events fulfill those criteria involve categorization, labeling, and classification of phenomena. While resolving definitional issues is often required in moral deliberation, disputes over the meaning or classification of terms do not necessarily arise from conflict over normative principles.

To formulate defensible goals in public affairs, therefore,

individuals must grapple with empirical and definitional, as well as moral or value, issues. Research skills in the collection, organization, and interpretation of data are required to determine, for example, the extent of housing code violations in a neighborhood or discriminatory practices in a public agency. To predict probable effects of proposed policies for dealing with such problems requires similar research capability. It is through concern for critical thinking, problem solving, disciplined thought, or inquiry that educators have already articulated various conceptions of research skills (see, for example, Massialas and Cox, 1966; Crabtree, 1967; Hunt and Metcalf, 1968; Beyer, 1971; Chapin and Gross, 1973; Fraenkel, 1973). Their models frequently elaborate on such steps as defining a problem, proposing a solution (hypothesis), testing the solution (hypothesis) through collection and interpretation of evidence, and reaching a conclusion. The same models may offer systematic conceptions of research and problem solving, but their utility in guiding social policy research is limited.

Such conceptions of inquiry, at least as proposed for social studies curriculum, often aim at questions that interest social scientists and historians, or at abstract notions of critical thinking, but not at questions of policy that interest the activist.[4] Important distinctions between discipline-oriented and social policy research should be made. In this regard, Coleman (1972b) argues:

1. Action research is initiated not by an intellectual problem aimed at theory building in a discipline, but by interests outside the discipline. The ultimate product, therefore, is not a "contribution to knowledge," but a social policy modified by research results.

2. The policy researcher needs to translate research questions generated for action purposes into questions that can be managed by a discipline, but that can be answered in a form meaningful to the outside client, as well as the scholar.

3. For policy research, it is better to base conclusions on partial information available at the time an action must be taken than it is to wait for complete information not yet available.

---

4. Kaplan (1964) and others who analyze the nature of scientific inquiry refer to "logic in use" as the intellectual process actually used by the scientist in daily work versus "reconstructed logic," a portrayal of process that may be deduced from finished scientific work or formal reporting of findings. Since inquiry models proposed by educators are usually exercises in reconstructed logic, they may give misleading notions of scientific inquiry.

4. Because of value preferences that orient policy research and that may suppress "undesirable" results, special "corrective" devices, such as the commissioning of more than one research group under auspices of different interested parties and an independent, adversarial review of research results are required to ensure valid results.

5. Certain stages of policy research lie in the world of action, and the researcher can legitimately advocate that research be conducted in accord with personal values; other stages lie within the disciplinary realm, and the researcher must abide by disciplinary values of objectivity that make certain types of advocacy inappropriate.

These points should lead us to develop new research or inquiry skills appropriate for citizen action. Consider the problem of collecting evidence or information, a rather obvious step in the research process. Inquiry models are too general to provide guidance about the particular evidence one ought to seek on specific issues or where one might find it. Because of the significance of information not readily available to, or even deliberately withheld from, the public, the social policy researcher needs at times to master "tricks of the trade" more characteristic perhaps of the muckraking journalist or private detective than of the scientific scholar.

Of course, even skilled policy researchers may be unable to demonstrate unequivocal consequences of specific policies. The "facts" are frequently contradictory or inconclusive, as has been shown by attempts to assess effects of interracial bussing on pupil achievement, the effects of smoking marijuana on health, or the effects of welfare payments on individual economic initiative. Skills in social policy research aid students in dealing with empirical issues relevant to public policy, but they do not guarantee the discovery of definitive answers leading to consensus. There have been some efforts to define specific skills required for various types of social research, but further delineation of curriculum appropriate for this area is necessary.[5]

---

5. See, for example, *Where It's At* (1970 est.), Jones (1971), Community Research and Publications Group (1972), Ross (1973), Marian *et al.* (1973), Michael (1974), Community Press Features (1974). Merelman (1971) outlines four components of policy thinking: moral thought, cause-effect thought, sociocentrism, and imaginative thinking. These are seen as general cognitive capacities rather than specific techniques of social research, but studies on the development of such capacities in children at different ages can guide our notions of specific skill development.

Working for Support of Goals

Skills in moral deliberation and social policy research should help a person decide what position to take: whether to support or oppose a ban on nonreturnable bottles, a guaranteed minimum income, a student bill of rights, or a particular candidate. Having taken a stand and arrived at a goal, the next step is to gain support so that it can become public policy. When there has been a sound ethical and empirical justification for policy goals, further efforts should be devoted primarily to gaining support for them.[6] That aspect of curriculum aimed at helping students muster support should provide knowledge of political-legal process, advocacy skills, knowledge of and skills in group dynamics, and practical skills in organization, administration, and management.

Knowledge of Political-Legal Process

One must know where in the matrix of institutions, at what times and in what manner, to direct efforts at gaining support for policy goals. Two general channels of influence are available. The first, and the one central to most conceptions of representative democracy, is to place in positions of power people who seem to agree with one's specific positions or one's general principles. This obviously requires exerting influence on the outcomes of elections and appointments to key positions in government. Also, and perhaps more important, one must attempt to affect the selection of leadership in sectors that influence government; for example, in business, organized labor, churches, professional associations and issue-oriented pressure groups. This might be called the *power-base approach,* for it attempts to establish effective representation in the proper circles as the main vehicle for implementing preferred policies. The strategy includes collective action in electoral politics, in the internal power structures of membership organizations, and in community organization efforts to create new centers of power.

It is also necessary to persuade persons already in power to support or oppose specific policies in accord with one's wishes. This

---

6. This is not to imply that in this stage of activism the ends justify the means or that any method of implementing one's goals is justifiable. Responsibility for moral deliberation is continuous, everlasting, and must be directed at any actions (even if they be seen as means to good ends) that raise ethical problems.

Agenda for Curriculum Development

might involve influencing a legislator to vote for a specific bill, persuading a pressure group to devote its resources to lobbying against administrative action, persuading a government agency to launch an investigation or to take legal action, persuading a bureaucrat to fund a project. This channel might be called the *direct policy approach*, for it aims more immediately at the enactment or repeal of specific policy by influencing appropriate existing power bases. Both the power-base approach and the direct policy approach require considerable knowledge of the dynamics of power in a community and within organizations.

An activist must become familiar with the formal and public "rules of the game." Examples might include how a bill becomes a law, how persons are nominated and elected to certain offices, which agencies have jurisdiction over certain matters, how decisions of officials can be appealed, how policy priorities and budgets are established within groups and agencies, to whom officials are legally accountable, what regulations govern the expression of citizen opinion or protest. Courses in social studies have traditionally tried to teach some of these aspects of the political-legal process, but topics in electoral politics at the national level tend to dominate such instruction to the exclusion of local affairs that may be more important in the lives of students. Students may be more interested in lines of authority within a school system than those within the federal government. Their exercise of influence might require a knowledge of how the school budget is created, how a juvenile might file a complaint with the police department, what local agencies would have to approve a publicly financed, but youth-managed mental health clinic. Knowing the formal or public rules that govern political-legal process does not guarantee successful exercise of influence, but such knowledge is crucial at certain times during a campaign.

Equally important, and virtually ignored in secondary curriculum, is knowledge about informal, less public channels of influence. To win support for one's objectives in a community or within an organization, knowledge of the "real" as opposed to the "formal" configuration of power is needed: groups and individuals that are potential allies and enemies on various issues; individuals and groups that have the most and least resources in people, money, and bargaining power; ways in which an association with certain individuals and groups might require modification of one's goals; procedures that can be taken privately, behind the scenes, to win support without escalating a point into a controversial public issue; how the outcome of a specific campaign can be affected by other community affairs. While much of the knowledge to be gained on informal, less publicized aspects of political-legal process may be idiosyncratic to specific issues and local communities, helpful information designed for a nationwide audience is available in some curriculum projects, in exposés and case studies of political events, and in handbooks for citizen action.[7]

Advocacy Skills

Knowledge of political-legal process helps to identify individuals and groups whose support is required to achieve one's goals. These persons, seen perhaps as targets for advocacy, must be persuaded to offer endorsements, votes, money, and active participation. Effective persuasion or advocacy has two general dimensions. One must offer for public scrutiny an argument that proposed actions, policies, or candidates are consistent with principles of justice and human dignity and that they constitute the most reasonable choices among possible alternatives. A systematic case, backed by evidence, logical consistency, and thorough analysis of the problem must be made. The message might be articulated through prepared argument in speeches, debates, written testimony, pamphlets, or letters, as well as spontaneous conversation and face-to-face organizing. This can be considered the rational, jurisprudential face of advocacy.

Providing a rational defense of one's cause in terms of principles of justice and community well-being does not, however, suffice to win support in political struggle. It must also be shown that proposed actions meet felt needs, values, and preferences of particular constituencies whose support is sought. Recognizing the importance of appeal to special interests within a community and to emotion as well as to intellect, this dimension of advocacy is concerned with creating messages that specific audiences want to see and hear and building slogans, symbols, and images that elicit feelings of identification and enthusiasm, not simply cognitive assent. Effective advocacy

---

7. Examples in these respective categories are Ratcliffe (1970), Ridgeway (1970), and Ross (1973). Exposés and journalistic accounts of the "realities" of political-legal process exist in abundance. A thorough review, selection, and cataloging of them into a bibliography appropriate for the thrust of this curriculum is needed.

Agenda for Curriculum Development

at an emotional level that appeals to special interests can be advanced further, perhaps, by using skills developed for public relations, market research, or the communications media, rather than by using adversarial skills to construct a tight substantive argument. Persuasive messages usually combine aspects of each dimension of advocacy, and elements from courses in speech, journalism, mass media, rhetoric, legal reasoning, public relations, and advertising can be helpful in developing advocacy skills.

Group Process Knowledge and Skills

One major lesson to be learned when studying influence in political process is the significance of groups. Individuals usually exert influence only to the extent that they can gain support from appropriate groups and to the extent that those groups can cooperate in pursuing a political strategy in an efficient and unified manner. The active citizen must decide how to affiliate with and participate in groups. Having chosen to act on a particular issue, for example, should one form a new organization or join an existing one? Within an organization, membership can be open or selective. A group establishes some system of governance and decides how explicit or formal to make it. And, of course, a group also chooses which issues to attack and which constituencies to represent. It is unfortunate that the school curriculum rarely addresses these problems. The model of citizenship participation is too often based on a myth of individual action when the strategy of collective group action is usually more effective.

Even though proven principles for maximizing group effectiveness have not been discovered, we should, nevertheless, continue to search for guidelines potentially useful to the student activist. Writings of activists and social scientists dealing with group work and community organization can be helpful.[8] One approach to instruction might outline alternative methods for resolving crucial problems of membership, internal authority, and division of responsibility within groups. Another approach might focus on solidarity as a central problem and evaluate various possible principles. For example, group

---

8. A thorough search for appropriate literature in this area should be made, but, as examples, the works of Thelen (1954), Alinsky (1971), Holden (1973), and Cox et al. (1974) seem relevant.

goals phrased in general terms can obscure fundamental disagreement among members about specific objectives, and, to build solidarity, these should be clarified early in the group's life. Also, projects that require sacrifice, struggle, and interdependence of participants enhance feelings of solidarity within a group. Another unit could address special problems in organization for groups trying to help others. Such groups must examine the extent to which potential recipients need to be involved in defining the goals and strategy of the group itself. Students might consider case studies of different approaches to group organization, discuss their apparent strengths and weaknesses, and search for analogues in their own experience. Students need not memorize a set of sacred principles on group organization, but they should examine guidelines put forth by experienced workers as keys to productive group work.

Inquiry about principles of group organization should be supplemented by attention to interpersonal behavior within the group, for, without a certain degree of trust and openness among group members, it is impossible to mount the collective effort necessary to exert influence. Students may need explicit identification of the interpersonal skills and sensitivities required for cooperation. Instruction might be offered, for example, on such topics as listening to the emotional as well as the literal content of conversation; asking persons directly for clarification of their views and feelings, rather than making untested assumptions from indirect cues; summarizing and synthesizing individual contributions to form a group position; how to ask for and offer help; the importance of giving and receiving criticism to help the group achieve its mission, rather than to satisfy personal emotional needs that might conflict with the mission.

Such topics indicate the relevance of interpersonal sensitivity to the exercise of political influence and demonstrate the need to consult literature in that general field.[9] This is not to endorse all forms of sensitivity training. Programs that teach the giving of unconditional warmth and trust to all, that focus exclusively on the reduction of anxiety, or that assign analysis of interpersonal dynamics a higher priority than substantive policy or task completion might actually reduce the group's political effectiveness. Group work aimed

---

9. Possible directions for specific instruction in this area are implied in the work of Miles (1959), Schein and Bennis (1965), Luft (1970), Schmuck and Schmuck (1971).

toward therapy or new approaches to personal fulfillment may have a proper place in public education, but the interpersonal skills we seek here are those necessary for carrying out task-oriented group efforts that increase the individual's ability to exert influence in public affairs.

Organization-Administration-Management Skills

This category refers to the nuts and bolts of citizen action. When is the right time for door-to-door canvassing? Would a mail or phone campaign be more effective? How soon should we contact the press and what should we tell them? Could we raise more funds through a bake sale or by soliciting special donations? Should we accept the man's word or press him to sign a statement? One must know how to plan a course of action and divide it into sequential steps, how to facilitate communication, how to set agendas for meetings, how to use parliamentary procedure, how to keep accurate financial records, how to use the yellow pages. Because the knowledge and skills needed by a student depend so much upon specific issues and situations, it may be difficult to create curricula suited to a nation-wide audience on some of these matters. Some advice, on the other hand, might be applied widely. For example, to give the impression of a large crowd of supporters, hold public meetings in relatively small rooms; to avoid co-optation, send at least two representatives from your group to meet with adversaries; make demands specific and indicate a date by which you expect a reply; since side issues will sometimes gain you more support or opposition than the central issue (police brutality gave peace and civil rights workers much support, but long hair or certain styles of expression lost them much support), take their effects into account in planning strategy; have a plan for reminding people of the jobs and responsibilities they have agreed to undertake.

Organization-administration-management skills touch on diverse topics, and perhaps they should be further classified as they apply to different types of action: running electoral campaigns; organizing public protest actions such as marches, demonstrations, boycotts, sit-ins, or strikes; encouraging popular lobbying efforts through petitions, letter writing, or testifying; working "quietly" to exert influence "behind the scenes" without creating a public uproar over your position. Each of these might require a separate set of skills or different hints for success that could become part of an organization-management handbook. The handbook could contain not only helpful suggestions, but also exercises for practicing certain skills, and, as students became involved in action, they could consult the handbook for material relevant to their particular project. Several sources have already outlined skills in these areas.[10]

It has taken several pages to outline the types of knowledge and skills which presumably would assist individuals and groups in exerting influence in public affairs. Does it seem that only a superhuman being could develop all of this competence? Have we not suggested that a social scientist, a moral philosopher, a legal advocate, a political journalist, a professional group worker, and an organizer-administrator all be combined in the average citizen? Such an ambitious design would be futile. To avoid such an interpretation, it is important to remember that the model is aimed toward creating an agenda for curriculum development, not a list of competencies for all students. The apparent impossibility of teaching all such skills to a single individual should further confirm that the exercise of influence must be tied to participation in groups and that effective group action requires division of labor. All persons cannot be expected to do all things. Some people have more knowledge and skills than others in each of the categories, and some citizens may choose to "specialize" in one or a few of the areas of competence. To say that a group of people wishing to exert influence should have the competencies we mention represented within it is not, therefore, to say that all persons must be skilled in all areas. And yet, as an ideal, we must hold that the more of these skills an individual can master, the greater is that person's ability to exert influence.

Resolving Psycho-Philosophic Concerns

The agenda up to this point has proposed some relatively specific areas of competence as requisites to effective citizen action. It is possible, however, that a person who is capable of formulating a rationally defensible position and who has keen insight on how to win

---

10. Oppenheimer and Lakey (1964), Huenefeld (1970), Lurie (1970), *Where It's At* (1970 est.), Kahn (1970), O. M. Collective (1971), Jones (1971), McKay (1971), Nader and Ross (1971), Wisconsin Youth for Democratic Education (1972), Gardner (1972), Allen *et al.* (1973), Ross (1973), Greene (1973), Massachusetts Advocacy Center (1974). The Appendix includes names of organizations that can supply further information.

support may yet be unable to act or may act in counterproductive ways. Failure to exert influence in such a case could not be explained by pointing to deficiencies in personal competence. The question, instead, is: Why did the person fail to use his or her competence? This section is based on the belief that using one's competence effectively depends largely upon how one resolves a number of concerns or dilemmas likely to confront active and potentially active citizens. These psycho-philosophic concerns may in a sense explain reasons for or causes of citizen apathy or unproductive action.[11] Some citizens are ineffective because they resolve the dilemmas in politically inappropriate ways. For others, the dilemmas create such ambiguity, stress, or anxiety that they cannot act at all. The general goal for curriculum is to prevent students from becoming immobilized by these concerns and to help them work toward resolutions that enhance rather than inhibit their ability to exert influence.

Because issues presented here have received virtually no attention in literature on citizen action or citizenship education, this section represents perhaps the most novel contribution of the book. More attention is paid to exposition of, rather than proposed solutions for, these concerns, and, in contrast to previous sections, the curriculum implications here are necessarily more general. While these concerns may seriously impede student exercise of influence in public affairs, their resolution does not seem to lie in acquiring the type of technical competence implied in areas already discussed. Where appropriate, the concerns should become explicit subjects for instruction and individual counseling, and curriculum must be designed accordingly. We cannot at this stage, however, prescribe a body of specific knowledge or a set of skills that will enable students to resolve these matters successfully.

Commitment and Openness

A number of issues can be subsumed under this heading. An activist must have confidence that his or her position is "correct." One must be committed to pursue the goal, undaunted by attempts of adversaries or skeptics to find error or to predict failure. On the

---

11. The extent to which citizens are consciously aware of these concerns has not been determined through quantitative research. They are proposed here as an initial taxonomy, based on my observation of young and adult activists and on my personal experience in trying to exert influence. Further reflection might well lead to a reformulation.

other hand, one must remain receptive to criticism, to new information, to alternative interpretations, so that action can be intelligently adapted to the demands of the environment. The complexity of the problem attacked and the inevitable fact that almost all action is based on incomplete information must be recognized. Refusal to act until all the evidence is in or until a proposed action has been proven correct beyond question is tantamount to inaction because possibilities for continued study of social problems are infinite. Literature on personality probably recognizes in this concern an aspect of "tolerance for ambiguity."

Taking decisive action in the face of uncertainty is especially difficult for those who wish to "keep all options open" or who feel that "the grass is always greener." Such individuals tend to feel that, by committing themselves to a certain course of action, they may miss out on something else that might come along. This ambivalence is seen in those who rarely finish a book but taste small parts of many; in persons who never pursue a hobby in any sustained, continuous way but dabble in several. The person who attempts to learn what he or she wants or what he or she is committed to by continuous superficial exploration of alternatives may never become committed to anything. Some psychological findings suggest that commitment or sustained involvement develops only if one actually takes a plunge, heavily investing oneself in a cause or activity (Kanter, 1972). Erikson's (1959) notion of a psycho-social moratorium is an attempt to recognize the developmental need for a period that allows for both a certain amount of ambivalent dilettantism and total personal investment and commitment in a focused direction.

In many situations the activist must have enough perseverance to work, in the face of apparently overwhelming odds, on projects that last many days, months, or years. Feedback on the results of one's actions is often delayed far into the future, and praise, recognition, and approval are infrequent rewards for one's work. This suggests that the activist needs courage and strength to sustain a long, arduous battle. Since refusal to try or giving up simply because failure is predicted can become a self-fulfilling prophecy, the activist must remain committed, even in the face of serious obstacles. On the other hand, energy must not be wasted on efforts that cannot succeed even with total commitment. Because human energy is limited, one has to be selective in undertaking projects, choosing those where success seems feasible.

Another manifestation of the problem of balance between commitment and openness is the conflict between systematic planning and organized anticipation versus flexibility and spontaneity. Present-oriented persons have difficulty planning for future contingencies. Some are extremely cautious about excessive planning, fearful of becoming slaves to structure, and unable to respond properly to circumstances as they arise. Others, who prefer systematic planning for all contingencies, find a casual, play-it-by-ear approach too unorganized and ineffective. The art is to arrive at some balance that incorporates the advantages and avoids the pitfalls of each orientation.

Persons versus Causes and Institutions

To influence public policy, one must obviously relate to individual persons—compatriots, adversaries, potential supporters and opponents, and persons important to the activist (parents, friends, spouses, children) who may not be directly involved in the issues. In the heat of social struggle interpersonal relationships are a frequent source of stress. How such problems are resolved can affect the interpersonal life of the activist. Because they affect the citizen who is acting, interpersonal relationships can thereby affect institutions or policies that the citizen seeks to change.

Reluctance to become involved in public affairs may sometimes be traced to a belief that such involvement almost inevitably brings with it some deterioration in interpersonal relations, or at least a lack of attention to the needs of each human being as a special person. There is the danger that, in the midst of social causes, people become objectified: adversaries become targets to defeat, replace, or blame; supporters become means to an end, that is, votes, dollars, or followers. The attempt to achieve a social goal (stopping a war, passing an equal rights law, lowering taxes) in the most rational, efficient way often obscures the personal human needs of adversaries and supporters alike. Given the conviction that every human being deserves moral respect as a unique person, we are warned that this basic value can be undermined through objectification; people become cogs in a larger struggle. One extreme remedy is to suggest that, rather than concentrating on problems of policy or institutional change, all people invest their energy into becoming humane and understanding toward each person they encounter. If everyone did, it is argued, there would be virtually no need to worry about equitable public policies.

This plea to focus more directly on the quality of interpersonal relationships than on matters of institutional policy can be explained psychologically. For adolescents, identification with particular persons outside the family may be critical in the development of identity. If a major developmental task is the working out of interpersonal relationships among peers and adults, then we would expect adolescents' choice of causes to be a result of their feelings about certain people, and we would expect them to focus primarily on the quality of interpersonal relationships as opposed to the manifest social cause for which they work. Concentrating upon personal relationships carries the benefit of providing immediate feedback and reinforcement as to "how one is doing"—a psychological reward that abstract causes or institutions cannot offer so directly.

For a variety of reasons, then, the thoughtful activist should become sensitive to the "human" aspects of attempting to influence public affairs. If one is overly responsive to personal needs, however, progress toward achieving one's goal can be retarded. There is always a danger that personal respect for an adversary might result in the incorporating of enough of the adversary's position to co-opt one's own position. Then, instead of working toward the goal or policy originally favored, one begins to support the former adversary, or at least to tone down opposition. Also, the activist might show such respect for the feelings of supporters and colleagues, such a desire to resolve harmoniously all questions of interpersonal tension, that it becomes impossible to mobilize group activity to complete a task. A possible extreme result of becoming sensitive to individual personal needs is that these receive so much attention that colleagues no longer feel united in a common cause, except possibly for improved human relations among themselves.

The point of these observations is to support neither a "person-oriented" nor a "cause-oriented" approach, but to indicate that those who wish to exert influence in public affairs are likely to face this dilemma. In spite of possible hazards, the activist must not allow commitment to the cause to overshadow sensitivity to people as individual humans. This sensitivity, necessary as a basic moral duty, also increases effectiveness. The activist must not, on the other hand, allow concern for personal needs and harmonious interpersonal relationships to deter progress toward justifiable public policy.

Agenda for Curriculum Development

Use of Power

Scope of action. An activist makes choices about the use of power. Given an almost infinite number of issues but limited time and resources, a person can take an active stand on only a few issues. If one wishes to be active in organizations that attack a variety of issues, participation must necessarily be limited. Selecting those issues and organizations in which to make a personal investment is troublesome for those who see dozens of worthy causes and are reluctant to accept the fact that, in order to work for some, they must deliberately choose to neglect others. However difficult the choices, priorities must be established, or limited power is diffused too widely to exert any influence. In addition to setting priorities for the type of issues to pursue (for example, peace, consumer protection, juvenile rights, environment, racism), one must also decide about the scale of objectives. Unattainable goals are frustrating. It is often better to concentrate on immediate, local problems than on those of global proportions. Rather than trying to regulate profit in the paper industry, it might be more effective to try to persuade a local school to increase its use of recycled paper. Yet, smaller, more manageable, short-term issues should never obscure the ultimate goal. A person who attempts to pass national legislation requiring use of recycled paper without first gaining the support of neighbors will probably not succeed. On the other hand, if all one's efforts are spent trying to persuade a stubborn neighbor, laws will never be changed.

Leader-follower roles. A second problem in the use of power is the extent to which the activist sees himself, or herself, as a leader or a follower. The general image of a person attempting to exert influence conveys a notion of assertiveness and leadership, yet it is absurd to expect that all students will become charismatic leaders. Besides, leadership requires a variety of styles and contexts. Some persons may lead small-group committees; others, mass participation activities. Some may provide intellectual leadership on substantive policy matters; others may deal with interpersonal relations. Dilemmas related to leading and following do, therefore, manifest themselves in different contexts for different individuals. Those inclined to lead must be careful not to deny power and responsibility to those who follow, for movements totally dependent upon one person are ultimately doomed to fail. Conversely, those inclined to follow must feel enough of an investment in the task so that they do not accept orders blindly, but assert their own power independently. Because young people are particularly sensitive to arbitrary authority, especially to peers exercising power over each other, the activist must continually examine the way in which he or she uses power within a project. Neither doing it all alone nor letting others do it is satisfactory. Functional authority patterns are crucial to a group's success, and they are important topics for group discussion as well as issues for individual private reflection.

Another manifestation of the leader-follower problem can be seen in the contrast between a *service-maintenance* versus a *change* orientation in the use of power. With a service-maintenance orientation, persons and institutions invite the assistance of an activist who attempts to please the client or recipient. Examples include volunteer work at a prison, Head Start centers, or homes for the elderly. In contrast, a change orientation requires that the activist attempt to persuade a recipient to accept something the recipient did not formerly support. Recipients or targets of change-oriented action often resist the independent, uninvited agenda that the activist wishes to implement. Examples here include student attempts to have a school board adopt a student bill of rights or to abolish grading. Usually advocacy of public policy is not considered a "service" by those to whom proposals and protests are addressed; instead, it is seen as a struggle by some to persuade others to change their ways. This is not to imply that change cannot be induced through a service-maintenance orientation. Tutoring programs may change students, Peace Corps and VISTA volunteers may change living conditions, and volunteers for the park department may clean up the parks, but these kinds of changes are intended to service the interests of hosts. In contrast, the crusades of a Ralph Nader are perceived, at least initially, as contrary to the interests of the target of the action.

The service-maintenance orientation implies the role of follower (one caters to the needs of others), while the change orientation suggests more independent leadership (one attempts to influence or guide others). A transactional interpretation of power, however, can avoid the pitfalls of placing activism into any one of these categories exclusively. Action can be viewed not as a one-way process (I help you, or I change you), but as a process in which activist and recipient or target of action grow mutually. The activist in this role suspends enough of his or her agenda to listen to and respond to the needs of the client or target, on the assumption that the activist will benefit. Yet the activist does not become the total servant of the recipient's agenda, for it is also assumed that the recipient will benefit from exposure to the activist's goals. The purpose of action in the transactional sense is synergetic growth, not a one-dimensional, cause-effect result.[12]

The power to hurt. A third problem arises when the activist must use power in ways that inevitably "hurt" others. An organization has limited funds and can hire only one staff member. If there are ten well-qualified applicants for the job, all of whom desperately need the income, nine must be turned away. Decisions on priority items in a budget illustrate another choice to give resources to some people and to deny them to others. Adolescents who have the power to govern in alternative schools often show a reluctance to use power over their fellows. Many are not even satisfied with a system where the majority rules, because they feel no person or group should exert any power over another. In addition to a reluctance to make policy that may deny some people their wishes, adolescents often will not participate in enforcing policy if it involves prescribing penalties or sanctions. With all the rhetoric about "power to the people," and student participation in governance, we must recognize that actual attainment of such power poses continuing dilemmas, as the activist must decide who is to benefit the most from the use of power. This issue also relates to problems discussed earlier as "Persons versus Causes and Institutions."

Integrity

A persisting dilemma for many activists is how to continue to work toward a goal without "selling out" or violating one's integrity. This issue takes many forms, and it is felt with varying degrees of severity. A person may feel strongly that a public act is wrong and want to denounce it harshly, yet realize that, to exert influence in appropriate places, one may have to suppress expression of certain feelings. In bargaining situations, one must decide whether to stand firm and press for all justifiable demands, or to compromise on some

---

12. For a more thorough treatment of this problem, see Freire (1970), and Hampden-Turner (1970).

issues for the sake of victory on others. Should one work for a candidate who, on the one hand, fails to measure up to standards, but who, on the other, seems preferable to all the alternatives? To preserve one's personal image and credibility, an activist may agree to do things that he would otherwise never do (cut his hair and dress conservatively or attend meetings or social functions he despises). Another may participate in volunteer work which she feels to be poorly managed, yet withhold criticism if she feels it would have a destructive effect on the ultimate goal.

Successful resolution of such problems requires more than the advice that "compromise is often necessary." The active citizen may face demands that entail modification of strongly held objectives representing profound philosophical and moral commitments. To uphold one's principles in the face of opposition, therefore, should not necessarily be considered inflexible rigidity, a false attempt to save face or honor, or even "impractical politics." When a specific compromise is seen as asking the activist to violate that part of oneself which constitutes the "sameness and continuity" (Erikson, 1960) that defines one's very existence, a question of political strategy becomes inextricably entwined with the very personal question, "Who am I?" In this sense, the question of compromise can have deep psychological and philosophical significance. If curriculum is to assist a person in exerting influence in public affairs, it must help in examining compromises to determine which seem reasonable and necessary for achieving policy goals and which involve serious threats to, or violations of, one's personal identity that perhaps should not be risked.

Personal Motives and Social Justifications

Although we recommend that the citizen rationally justify attempts to influence public policy, we also recognize that formal, rational justification is not a sufficient *explanation* for behavior. "Why" a person becomes involved can also be explained with reference to personal needs that may seem irrelevant to formal policy justification. These personal needs or motives can be described in a number of ways, and some may lend themselves to conscious examination more readily than others. We might ask, for example, if involvement in action might be meeting the activist's personal needs at the expense of other people: Might my attempt to help others actually represent a need of mine to manipulate or control them, or to foster their dependence on me, or to demonstrate my superiority? We must also wonder whether the extent of one's involvement is determined mainly by a consideration of what is currently popular: Might my involvement in this campaign be based on a transient sense of excitement, being part of an "in" issue, rather than sticking with a more permanent commitment that may not always attract attention?

In one project we inquired about students' views of the main purpose behind their social action efforts. For some students, personal learning is the major purpose. They become involved primarily because they want to develop individual skills, gain knowledge about specific problems, broaden their understanding of people with whom they have had no previous contact, gain information on possible vocational interests, and so forth. Since the individual student sees the activity as contributing to individual education or growth, the main motive behind participation in this sense is *self-education*.[13]

Other students, by outward appearance more "militant" and committed to a cause, see the completion of a task or project as the major purpose of their activity. The object is to persuade the council to rezone the land, to publish a group newspaper, to elect a candidate, to raise money for the poor, to organize a peace rally, or to provide reliable volunteer service. Though students feel they learn while carrying out their projects, self-education is seen not as the central focus, but as a fortunate by-product of the activity. The central mission is to complete a successful project, to produce results, a motive we label *task completion*.

Many students see neither self-education nor task completion as the major purpose of their involvement in a social action project. Their goal may be simply to escape the routine, the pressures, and the demands of ordinary courses; to find a chance to relax or to rap with friends informally; to get away from adults; or to be "entertained" by guest speakers or field trips. Such concerns can be summarized under the term *recreation*.

Finally, some students seem to have no identifiable motivation

---

13. Gottlieb (1974) found that younger, in contrast to older, VISTA volunteers had, mixed with their altruism, "an important developmental need to find out who they were and what the outside world was really like." Social action thus provides an opportunity for "self-discovery," the pursuit of which may sometimes run contrary to the ostensible purpose of the action (i.e., assisting a community).

behind involvement in social action. They do not seem to be interested in either learning, completing a project, or "having fun." Such students seem to pass through school mindlessly, without a sense of purpose, almost as if they were under anesthesia. They appear to be in a state of suspension from involvement or choice. The function of social action (or probably any other activity) for such a student is only another context for *hibernation*.

In exploring with students whether the social justification for one's involvement is compatible with personal motives, important contradictions might be discussed. A student whose primary motive is to learn something about political process may, in an electoral campaign, shun routine clerical work, feeling that she could learn more by participating in top-level policy discussions with "the heavies." In this case pursuit of personal motives might reduce chances of accomplishing the ostensible goal: winning the election. If possible contradictions are exposed, students can make more intelligent choices about the priority they wish to place on personal motives or social causes.

Personal motives might also be analyzed in terms of different roles that the activist may take. Some students are primarily concerned with helping others, often in a one-to-one relationship as in volunteer work in day-care centers, homes for the elderly, tutoring programs, and so forth. These we might call the humanitarians or "Good Samaritans." Others are primarily interested in fighting for something of direct benefit to themselves: securing a bill of rights for students, winning approval for an alternative school, trying to establish a cooperative student store. Because these students have a more tangible self-interest in the outcome of their work, they can be called "vested interest advocates." Finally, there are those who work for broader social causes: achieving world peace, developing a rational city plan, diminishing pollution, improving police-community relations. In these issues the activist often does not appear to have an immediate tangible personal stake; nor is the action designed to help a particular constituency. Activists in this category can be said to operate more in the role of "social planner" or "general citizen" working for the betterment of the community-at-large.

We can ask about motivations underlying such roles. Might the effort to engage in one-to-one personal helping situations be an attempt to escape the conflict and complexity involved in vested

Agenda for Curriculum Development

interest advocacy? Might extensive involvement in vested interest advocacy reflect insensitivity to needs of others, or lack of willingness to concern oneself with the total community? Might the social planner orientation involve an elitist desire to remain distant from the concrete, day-to-day needs of individual humans, and in some sense reveal a desire to control whole communities or institutions? Questions like these might help a person identify personal motives which, in addition to the social justification for an action project, help to explain one's own behavior.

The point of distinguishing between personal motives and social justifications is not to imply that action is contaminated or less legitimate when personal motives become apparent. Quite the contrary. It is hoped that the attempt to exert influence in public affairs will bring joy, recreation, humor, intimacy, adventure, and other personal benefits to the activist—benefits that go beyond the public justification for policy aims. The efforts of racial, ethnic, and religious groups to preserve cultural traditions illustrate how legitimate personal motivations can be pursued through advocacy for policies and candidates. Whether arguing for inclusion of black studies in a curriculum, or tax exemptions for church properties, the personal motivation here may rest in a feeling of responsibility to a heritage. The heritage derives its significance from the fact that it helps define for individuals the very meaning of their existence as unique human beings. As another example of personal benefits accruing through citizen action, Alinsky (1971) stresses that action projects be planned so that participants have a good time. He claims that failures of the radical new left in the 1960's can be explained in part by their lack of a sense of humor. Having fun in social action, according to Alinsky, is important not just because of its personal benefits, but also because it helps you win. Because the meeting of personal motives can serve to enhance or inhibit one's ability to exert influence in public affairs, these needs should be examined explicitly.

Implications

What are the implications for curriculum of the psycho-philosophic concerns raised thus far? There seem to be three general instructional tasks, depending upon students' needs. First, there are those who have probably not thought carefully about these issues and have, as a result, resolved them in ways that inhibit their ability to exert influence. Such persons may take extreme positions when faced with a dilemma. Some students resolve the commitment-openness dilemma, for example, by becoming so dogmatic (total commitment) that people do not listen to them. Others may choose never to give sustained effort to any problem because they wish to keep all options open (total openness). For these students, the task of curriculum is to introduce alternative perspectives and to show how extreme choices may destroy effectiveness. Second, there are students who have already become aware of alternative extremes on some dilemmas and have struggled with them, but they have become paralyzed by their inability to arrive at "perfect" solutions. One example would be a student who refuses to participate in an environmental cleanup because he claims it attacks only a symptom of the problem. He also refuses to participate in any effort to reform the economic system, which he calls the heart of the problem, because he feels the problem is too large and complex. For such students, curriculum must do more than identify the horns of the dilemma. It must work toward actual personal resolutions, admittedly imperfect, that will help the student act effectively. Third, and perhaps most important, the curriculum must recognize that citizen action is likely to evoke stress and anxiety arising from concerns of this sort, and it must offer emotional support that will help students find more satisfaction in acting, even with certain concerns unresolved, than in not acting at all. The extent to which curriculum would include individual psychological counseling, the study of classic philosophic issues, biographical studies of activists, or other matters is a problem for future development; it is discussed somewhat further in Chapter 4.

The major point of this section has been to move beyond commonplace observations that students are cynical and apathetic, that they feel too alienated or powerless to participate. We have suggested that the sources of such feelings may lie in particular concerns inherent in the process of exerting influence in public affairs and, because these concerns are "unresolvable" in any perfect sense, they create stress and anxiety for the active citizen. According to this analysis, the educational solution is not to convince youth to have more confidence in "the system," but to help them cope with stress arising from participation in that process. By proposing a set of psycho-philosophic dilemmas, we have pointed out some particular cognitive-emotional areas that deserve the educator's attention. Efforts to help students cope with these problems will, it is assumed, facilitate their ability to exert influence in public affairs.

The Agenda in Perspective

Before rushing to translate this agenda into actual materials, courses of study, and educational experiences for youth, we must recognize certain limitations. In trying to break down a general objective into specific components we have, in a sense, used Tyler's (1949) approach to curriculum planning—that is, a "competency-based" model. There are, however, both empirical and logical difficulties in reducing a general concept of ability into specific elements.

We have not systematically studied citizens successful in exerting influence in public affairs and discovered a set of attributes that differentiates them from persons unsuccessful in exerting influence. Neither can we argue that our proposed set of components is the *only* set leading to successful exercise of influence. There are no doubt alternative ways of classifying specific competencies in this area. Marsh (1973), for example, working with adolescents in a "community seminar," argued that involvement in public affairs requires taking risks. He hypothesized that the nature and extent of student involvement might be explained by willingness to take certain kinds of risks. Using this theory, risk taking could conceivably be a crucial sort of competence for such a curriculum. Another approach suggests that, instead of teaching a complicated set of skills and psychological processes, effort should be concentrated on consciousness raising: demonstrating to people the powerful personal consequences of certain social problems and dramatizing for them the need to act. This approach assumes that, if awareness and motivation are sufficiently heightened, people will develop on their own whatever more specific competencies may be necessary for effective action. A third way of organizing such a curriculum would be to note in our psycho-philosophic dilemmas a strong relationship with the Eriksonian crises of trust-mistrust, autonomy-shame and doubt, initiative-guilt, and industry-inferiority. Though Erikson's theory offers no prescriptions for the healthy resolution of such conflicts, one might reasonably view the successful handling of these issues as prerequisites for competent exercise of influence.[14]

It is possible that competencies should be defined not in a general way for all students, but more individualistically, depending upon students' developmental maturity and specific interests. Kohlberg and Mayer (1972) make a strong case against any curriculum not derived from developmental theory, but the curriculum implications of their work, or that of Piaget or Erikson, have yet to be clarified. Differences in ethnicity and social class might also be taken into account in attempts to specify areas of competency appropriate for different students. Dowtin (1973) and Worrill (1973), for example, in analyzing needs of black students, argue that the development of collective commitment and the mastery of certain concepts for viewing social reality should receive the highest priority. Steinitz *et al.* (1973) find that articulate white students from working-class families are highly motivated toward individual mobility but lack the social consciousness to risk economic security, which accompanies some forms of political involvement. Such students, if interested in activism at all, would probably have to be involved in projects where their individual vested interests could be pursued. More affluent, upper-middle-class students might, however, be more interested in altruistic forms of action.

Even if we could show logically and empirically the need for mastery of a specific list of competencies, there remains the problem that "the whole may be more than the sum of its parts." The skill of riding a bicycle involves more than a mastery of the separate components of steering, pedaling, braking, and balancing. The separate components must be put together in some special way that may be difficult, if not impossible, to describe and teach explicitly. We have been able to teach the acquisition of specific skills in dialogue on public issues (Newmann and Oliver, 1970), for example, but there is always the danger that students, while being able to perform separate skills in a technically acceptable manner (stating issues, summarizing discussions), will not "put it all together" in a way that indicates general ability in discussion of public affairs. It is hoped that dissection of a general ability into more specific components will inform us

---

14. I am grateful to Charles Slater (personal communication) for making direct connections between Erikson's framework and ours.

about the nature of interaction among components that leads to the "whole." Unfortunately, such discoveries have yet to be made about skills subsumed under the familiar educational objectives of critical thinking, disciplined inquiry, or rational choice making.

Continuing this chain of stipulations, suppose we could overcome all the difficulties posed thus far and produce a scheme showing how specific attributes interact so as to result in the general ability to exert influence in public affairs. This would provide student performance objectives for a curriculum, but it would still be insufficient. Competency objectives alone do not logically prescribe the need for any specific set of learning experiences. Identifying particular lessons and activities, as well as the content and methods likely to develop particular competencies, is essentially an empirical problem that can best be solved through vast experimental efforts in curriculum development, not through logical analysis.

There are broader social implications of competency-based models, especially when the models are used primarily to develop competent individuals.[15] Arguments can be made that, by focusing so much on individual competence, the schools are helping to reinforce destructive competition as students learn to equate education with demonstrating that one is "better" than others. By emphasizing individual progress and individual rights, competency-based models may be promoting socially irresponsible autonomy rather than collective cooperation. If self-worth is assessed almost totally in terms of what an individual can do, usually in an academic or technical sense that neglects human feelings and the quality of interpersonal relationships, personal alienation and isolation are exacerbated. If the purpose of education is at least partially to assist survival of the human species and if that requires a greater sense of interdependence and community at local, national, and international levels, then models of curriculum development should at least not impede progress in that direction. All too often a competency-based model can imply that individual benefits alone are the ultimate aim of learning. To the extent that this orientation diverts attention from the development

15. Although the prevailing trend lies in this direction, educational assessment need not focus exclusively on increased proficiencies for individual students. Wehlage, Popkewitz, and Hartoonian (1973) propose a scheme in which schools are held accountable for providing experiences or certain kinds of learning environments, but not directly for improving individual student competence.

of collective consciousness and responsibility, it is immoral and socially suicidal.

Finally, we must question the extent to which educators' deliberate intervention in peoples' lives can actually bring about increased competence in the areas specified. To the extent that human predispositions and capabilities are manifestations of universal patterns of maturation and development or of deeply ingrained personality traits or to the extent that they are genetically determined, deliberate intervention may be ineffective. Even if one assumes an almost infinitely malleable or teachable organism, the extent to which the educator lacks power to control the many environmental variables that affect what students learn further limits effectiveness in building prescribed competencies. The history of many previous efforts in curriculum and school reform should leave us with a sense of humility, but not a self-fulfilling hopelessness about our own ability to help people become more competent.

We have outlined an imposing agenda for curriculum. By discussing limitations of the approach, we provide a perspective that, rather than impeding the work, should move it forward. In a curriculum with different aims, there might be less reason to begin planning through a competency-based orientation. Curricula aimed primarily at teaching the academic disciplines, for example, can use as a guide to their content topics that are researched and taught by practicing scholars in universities. Our curriculum, however, puts forth a new objective (increased ability to exert influence in public affairs) that has no institutionalized, practicing professional community to offer guidance on what should be taught. In this frontier area, then, we face the challenge of defining or elaborating a conception of what seems to be involved in the ability to exert influence. While a competency-based model may resolve only insufficiently a number of important issues, it can, as shown here, be analytically useful in organizing our thoughts about specific components or targets for future curriculum development.

CHAPTER 4
Program Structure

Now we turn to problems of translating the curriculum model into an actual school program. Before taking the plunge into school practice and foisting untested ideas upon innocent students, it would be ideal to undertake a complete investigation of the many questions that the curriculum model alone cannot answer; for example, what specific curriculum and teaching interventions actually help a student resolve dilemmas of commitment-openness? Adequate research could, however, take many years, and, if schools had to postpone curriculum development until conclusive research answered all important pedagogical questions, curriculum development would come to a halt and schools would wait indefinitely for research to justify proposed programs. Schools must help initiate the needed research by supporting development of citizen action curricula. Fortunately some guidance is available in the experience of a number of youth participation projects already undertaken. Examples of such projects appear in the Appendix. While none of these has operated precisely on the conception of citizen action proposed here and none has produced research on how to implement components of our model, the experience does indicate major program issues that a proposed model must inevitably confront. This chapter includes recommendations on the place of citizen action in existing secondary programs, selection of students, administration-management, and the general instructional climate.

Much of the analysis here and in Chapter 5 is based on experience with a course, the Community Issues Program, piloted in Madison,

Wisconsin, from 1969 to 1971.[1] This course, which carried social studies credit, was available to students in grades nine through twelve as a full-year (1 credit) or a semester (1/2 credit) course. Enrollment was voluntary and varied from about twenty-five to seventy in a school of about eighteen hundred. It met in two-hour blocks, the last class periods of the day, on two days per week. With parents' permission, students were free to leave school during class periods. Although staff often accompanied students on their fieldwork in the community, this was not required. Students had considerable autonomy in the definition and selection of action projects, which occupied virtually all of the program's attention. Apart from a brief orientation and the presentation of periodic reports from each action group, there was no large-group instruction, and no common curriculum content was to be mastered by all students. Instead, most of the time was devoted to planning, executing, and evaluating student projects that involved community research, volunteer service, and social action. The staff consisted of two to three regular high school teachers, myself, and as many as six graduate students. Hourlong staff meetings before each class and occasional daylong staff retreats involved the staff in extensive deliberation about the program.

The exploratory nature of the program made systematic research into its effects on students impractical. Student evaluations were, however, generally quite positive. Because the emphasis was on student-initiated local projects, curriculum materials—a collection of community resources, handbooks, and information relevant to the students' projects—specific to those projects emerged. But this "curriculum" was not generalizable to other contexts. In other words, the course did not yield a curriculum package appropriate for dissemination to other schools; nor did it supply quantitative research on methods of teaching social action skills. The Madison course operated not from the curriculum model presented above, but from a more ambiguous notion of community involvement. Its major contri-

---

1. Madison is a city of about 170,000, with a nonwhite population of less than 5 percent. Its economy depends largely on employment in state government and education, and it is considered primarily an upper-middle-class, professional community. It is known for progressive politics and its scenic four lakes. Each of its four main high schools enrolls between two thousand and three thousand students, and the Board of Education has supported two alternative secondary schools. Though one could legitimately question the relevance of programs developed in this community for either inner-city or rural systems, issues confronted here have been and will be replicated in most metropolitan areas.

Program Structure

bution was to reveal many of the issues identified in this book and to stimulate development of the more systematic conception presented here.

Place of Citizen Action in the High School Curriculum

Having argued for citizen action curriculum as the highest priority in general education, we have not as yet specified an amount of time or any structure for implementation into existing secondary programs. Many schools already provide opportunities for student involvement in community affairs through extracurricular projects, independent study, and community-oriented assignments in regular courses (for example, environmental surveys in biology or preservation of historic sites in history). Through these opportunities some students, "doing their thing" in the community, gain a taste of limited aspects of exerting influence in public affairs, but the approaches reflect only a tangential concern for social action skills. The curriculum of many schools also includes formal courses of instruction relevant to our agenda on such topics as political behavior, public issues, the environment, or communication. There may also be a course in values or moral reasoning, and possibly opportunities for internships in the community. These isolated bits and pieces of instruction are appropriate to our model, but no school seems to have integrated or synthesized the potential contribution of such parts toward the central goal of increasing student ability to exert influence.

Some schools have developed a special single course in community involvement that gives the subject clearer academic legitimacy, especially when it is accepted as meeting part of the social studies requirement (or that of some other major) for graduation. But most single courses seem to be guided by objectives other than increased ability to exert influence in public affairs. (Recall the diverse purposes for community involvement outlined in the Introduction.) Even a full-year course aimed directly at this objective, however, offers an inadequate amount of time for developing the knowledge, skills, and attitudes called for in our conception of ability to exert influence.

Assume a four-year secondary school in which students take, on the average, four main courses at a time, each full-year course counting for one credit, with sixteen credits required for graduation. If one were to take our curriculum agenda seriously, the minimum amount of time required would be the equivalent of four year-long courses, that is, four credits or about one-fourth of the total graduation requirement. This citizen action work could also legitimately accomplish other learning objectives and earn credits in English, social studies, or other subjects, depending upon the nature of problems the student pursues. These credits could be distributed in various ways throughout the student's four-year program. Each student who elects the curriculum, however, should become involved at some phase for a significant amount of time and not be distracted by numerous other curricular obligations. To assure this, it would be advisable to require a major practicum experience consisting of at least two credits and occupying the student at least half time for a full year. The practicum would provide sustained, continuous participation in, and reflection upon, actual action projects in the community. While other aspects of the curriculum must also include practical experience and direct community involvement, the practicum would be distinguished by a long-term action experience occupying a central focus in the student's school program for one full year.

In the following section we suggest how aspects of some subjects currently taught in the secondary schools can be covered through components in the citizen action curriculum. Table 2 summarizes, for each part of the curriculum model, aspects of conventional subjects that could be taught through the citizen action curriculum and additional subjects from which the citizen action agenda might benefit. Subjects in the latter category are those containing a literature, set of skills, or substantive knowledge on which the activist might draw selectively, but which would in no sense indicate mastery of the subject itself. Parts of these subjects could be helpful in developing ability to exert influence, but development of that ability would not necessarily assist in the teaching of those subjects.

Moral deliberation. The rational justification of value choices may be considered one manifestation of "critical thinking" commonly stressed in subjects as diverse as social studies, English, science, or mathematics. Each of these areas emphasizes such cognitive operations as recognition of the assumptions behind an argument, identification of logical inconsistency, providing support for one's generalizations through deductive or inductive reasoning and evidence,

TABLE 2
Relationship of social action components to subjects in the curriculum

Social action component	Subject "covered"	Additional subjects that could contribute
Moral deliberation	Social studies[a] (English)	Philosophy Literature
Social policy research	Social studies (sciences, math)	Any subject relevant to the policy under consideration
Political-legal process	Social studies	Law Sociology
Advocacy	English (speech, journalism)	Law Public relations History
Group process	English Psychology	Sociology Social psychology Community organization
Organization-administration-management	None	Business management Accounting Labor relations
Psycho-philosophic concerns	None	History Philosophy Literature (biography) Religion Psychology Counseling

[a]Social studies refers collectively to history and the many social science disciplines (sociology, anthropology, political science, psychology, economics, etc.).

making distinctions between prescriptive, empirical, and analytic claims. Those advocates of rational inquiry concerned primarily with empirical or analytic skills might be better served under the social policy research component of our model. There is, nevertheless, an increasing emphasis on "values education" that, under this aspect of social action curriculum, could be responded to through the frameworks of Oliver, Shaver, Newmann, and Kohlberg. Such training, while most directly related to social studies content, could conceivably help to teach thought processes nurtured also in English, science, and mathematics.

Instruction in moral deliberation would accomplish more than cognitive skills or process goals. Students would study moral dilemmas faced by actual people in authentic historical and contemporary situations, and they would be confronted with classic issues and positions taken by laymen and professional commentators on such problems as universalism-relativism, utilitarianism, and free will-determinism. In this sense, students would also master selected content in social and intellectual history.

To say that social studies content and process would be covered through instruction in moral deliberation is not to say that social studies courses adequately teach moral deliberation. New curricula, with moral deliberation as a focus, must be developed. In addition to sources already mentioned, contributions in the field of ethical philosophy could be translated into curricula appropriate for secondary students. Literature that might otherwise be treated in English or drama, such as novels, short stories, biographies, plays, or poems, in which individuals deal with moral dilemmas would also contribute.

Social policy research. Moral deliberation addresses the prescriptive side of public affairs: What policies are good or right or ought to be supported on the basis of what values or normative principles? Resolving these problems also often requires answers to an empirical question: What have been the effects of policy X, or what are the likely effects of policy Y? Solutions to these descriptive or factual problems, given the limitations suggested, for example, by Coleman (1972), are a special challenge for the policy researcher. Topics in data collection, reliability and validity of measurement, experimental design, sampling, probability, statistics, and, more generally, inference itself, may help students interpret quantitative data in a way that will enable them to evaluate empirical generalizations about the effects of any given policy. Knowledge and skills represented by such topics emanate from the social sciences, the physical sciences, and mathematics. Curriculum development to be pursued in this area would depend upon each of these broad fields, but the form of instruction would probably emphasize social science research in its many and varied forms most directly.

Skilled *acquisition* of information, perhaps logically prior to skilled *interpretation*, would form a critical part of this component. Use of libraries, public records, original surveys, and the kinds of "digging" techniques used by creative journalists, private detectives, businessmen, and community organizers would be included. To the extent that such instruction serves to enhance the student's ability to obtain important information, it would be consistent with curriculum objectives in virtually all subjects.

Student involvement in particular issues would require that they learn substantive background in certain academic subjects. The study of water or air pollution, for example, might require mastery of some aspects of chemistry, physics, or biology. A project on the nutritional value of food in the school cafeteria might lead to knowledge in allied health fields. Projects dealing with poverty or welfare might profit from knowledge of selected aspects of economics. Such knowledge can be gained on an ad hoc basis as it becomes relevant to student concerns. The bits and pieces of knowledge acquired in these subjects are by no means a substitute for teaching them in their own right, apart from the concern for active participation in public affairs. It is important, however, to recognize that research on social policy matters also yields substantive knowledge and that teachers knowledgeable in relevant subjects can help students investigating policy questions.

Political-legal process knowledge. Knowledge about formal and informal aspects of political process is probably already being communicated in the many social studies courses (history, political science, government, problems of democracy, and others) that traditionally claim responsibility for citizen education. Unfortunately, such courses are rarely organized around the student's own exercise of influence, and, therefore, the "politics" taught is often judged to be of little use to the citizen. Courses in these subjects could, without violating the integrity of their discipline, revise their approach to focus more directly on case studies of actual attempts to exert influence within political-legal systems. Such studies need not cater to the immediate and occasionally trivial interests of students. The use of power can be examined through biographies and autobiographies of activists, the work of social scientists and muckraking journalists, and student-initiated research into local power structures.

While social studies content would obviously be "covered" through revised instruction on the political-legal process, social studies teachers would not be the only source of information. A variety of people in both the school and community could be helpful, depending upon their experience in public affairs. A physical education teacher active in environmental protection may be more helpful on the politics of that problem than the social studies teacher. An active feminist in the art department might be more helpful to young women working on "affirmative action" than the political science teacher. An attorney knowledgeable in local administrative law might know more about "politics" in the zoning department or city assessor's office than anyone on the school faculty. Instruction in the realities of political-legal process, especially at the local level, could in these ways benefit from the help of many outside the social studies faculty.

Advocacy skills. A persuasive case for a policy proposal rests upon a rational defense built through skills in moral deliberation and social policy research. If the case is to be effectively communicated, however, additional skills are required. The writing of briefs (reflecting a jurisprudential style of argument) and pamphlets, the preparation of speeches and testimony, strategic formal debate, and informal conversation aimed at winning support for one's cause are all important for disseminating proposals. The essential task here is the creative use of language to influence the intended audience. Learning advocacy skills would be equivalent to mastering the English language. Speech, debate, rhetoric, journalism, and law make major contributions to the development of advocacy skills. These could be further supplemented by selected approaches to the fields of broadcasting, public relations, media design, or even marketing. Alternative approaches toward persuasion in politics, law, and commerce, perhaps from a historical or anthropological perspective, might also assist skill development.

Group process knowledge and skills. This and remaining components in our citizen action model have analogues in conventional school subjects that are far less obvious than those discussed thus far. Some schools have courses which stress empathetic listening and interpersonal honesty within small groups, possibly through courses in psychology, English, or an interdisciplinary program in peer counseling. While such courses do not fit any standard mold, their common concern with more effective communication (not advocative in nature) places them in the English area also. This is not to claim that English curricula or teachers of English generally take this approach. It is merely to note that, if students were to learn interpersonal sensitivity and principles of group dynamics, their ability to communicate would improve. It would thus be legitimate to grant credit in English if some such designation had to be made.

One aspect of group process knowledge deals less with interpersonal behavior within groups and more with general principles applied to aggregates. Literature in sociology or social psychology is potentially useful as it relates to such topics as social cohesion, functions and roles in group task completion, advantages and disadvantages of alternative authority or leadership structures, generation of group commitment, approaches to conflict resolution. In addition, there are writings by labor organizers, social workers, and community organizers setting forth principles of successful group work. To develop this area of the curriculum requires considerable exploration into fields beyond those conventionally offered in the secondary school.

Organization-administration-management. Most of the rudimentary expertise in this area comes not from the study of subjects in the curriculum, but from actual experience in the exercise of influence. A plentiful supply of handbooks and a resource file of local experts can help students learn how to run a meeting, how to raise funds, how to publicize an event, how to keep records, or how to bargain with an adversary. While the study and mastery of such problems cannot readily be equated with any single aspect of the high school curriculum, helpful resources are probably available in any school. A journalism teacher might show students how to make arrangements with a printer. An accounting teacher might give advice on bookkeeping. A member of the teachers' union bargaining team might describe the bargaining process. Student experience in extracurricular activities can be helpful in learning to handle practical matters in action contexts (arranging a contract with a band to play for a local dance or soliciting financial contributions for costumes for a student play).

Psycho-philosophic concerns. This part of citizen action agenda is the most novel to secondary curriculum. Reflection on the problems of commitment-openness, persons versus causes and institutions, the use of power, integrity, and personal motives versus social justifications would, by no stretch of the imagination, serve to "cover" any subject already taught in school. To the extent that the purpose is to help students deal with sources of anxiety that may be unique to the activist role, the function may be similar to that of the school psychologist or the counselor. There is, however, no known curriculum or counseling process that teaches students how to resolve such issues in a way that maximizes their exercise of influence. One approach to the study of such problems would be to examine case studies of active persons, past and present, who seem to have faced such issues, encouraging students to compare their experiences with those of others. Teachers of history, political science, psychology, and literature could help locate such studies. Literature in philosophy and religion (dealing, for example, with cosmic issues regarding one's relationship to one's fellowman and the purpose of one's life on earth) can also be helpful in developing this aspect of the curriculum. Whatever approaches are used here should be well grounded in adolescent psychology, for this phase of the curriculum, more than any other, is intended to deal directly with sources of personal stress arising from attempts to make an impact in public affairs.

This review of the relationship between components of the social action agenda and conventional school subjects should not be seen as an attempt to justify the citizen action components on the ground that they help students learn conventional school subjects. Each component is better justified through its contribution to increased ability to exert influence in public affairs. Furthermore, each component could be justified on other grounds, independent both of citizen action and existing curricular aims. Moral deliberation could be justified with reference to Kohlberg and Mayer's (1972) philosophy of development as the aim of education. Group dynamics and psychophilosophic concerns could be justified through psychological theory on the nature of personal emotional growth. The major reason for cataloging our components in relation to familiar course topics is to show, first, how the curriculum might be implemented without totally disrupting existing credit requirements, and, second, to indicate fields of knowledge to which we might turn for help in the development of these components.

With this in mind, we offer an illustrative proposal for fitting the curriculum model into a secondary program. Assuming, as mentioned earlier, the need for a four-credit curriculum, a school could develop two one-credit courses and one two-credit practicum as follows:

Course A: "Taking a Stand: Moral Deliberation and Social Policy Research."
   One social studies credit.
Course B: "Winning Support: Persuasion and Group Work."
   One English credit.

Program Structure

Course C: "Practicum in the Exercise of Influence."
One-half social studies credit.
One-half English credit.
One "flexible" credit.

The practicum would place major emphasis on student projects, though fieldwork would also occur in courses A and B. Political-legal process knowledge, organization-administration-management skills, and psycho-philosophic concerns would be studied as they occur idiosyncratically in practicum projects, but materials and resources on these topics would be prepared in advance, ready to be used at appropriate times. The one flexible credit would be assigned to any subject for which, during the practicum work, the student demonstrated appropriate mastery: science, math, languages, home economics, health, depending upon the nature of the student's action project. Students would contract independently with teachers in appropriate subjects for the earning of such credit, and, depending upon school policy, this might be further apportioned into fractional credits.

"Taking a Stand" and "Winning Support" are recommended as prerequisites for the practicum. To ensure that they do not become isolated from making actual policy decisions and trying to win real support, they must include community involvement activity, for example, placing students in apprentice roles to adult activists or in volunteer work where policy issues and winning support are salient concerns. During the practicum, students would undertake projects where they would take more independent responsibility for influencing policy.

Because higher levels of maturity are required for effective practicum work, it should probably be restricted to the eleventh or the twelfth grade. Seniors might be especially interested in this opportunity to function more in an adult role. To allow for action projects related to the school itself, however, it should also be open to eleventh graders who could follow through on, and derive future benefit from, projects related to school life. Because of the cognitive sophistication required in moral deliberation and social policy research, we recommend that "Taking a Stand" generally not be offered below the eleventh grade, but "Winning Support" could probably be offered in grades ten through twelve.

These recommendations must be qualified by the realization that there is no conclusive empirical evidence to show that this is the best sequence for learning citizen action skills. The literature and experience that can be brought to bear on the question suggest, however, that the curriculum not be offered in a random fashion to students at any age and that these guidelines represent a best guess as to the point at which curriculum development in this area ought to begin. In prescribing prerequisites and grade-level criteria we risk excluding students who might otherwise benefit. We must, therefore, continually question the assumptions that lead to the requirements, and schools should create mechanisms for making fair exceptions to the guidelines. Interviews, examination of previous experience, and testing might demonstrate that a student is competent or mature enough to waive a prerequisite or grade-level requirement.

The recommended sequence does allow for considerable variation in student scheduling, as shown in Table 3. Mike completes the program in a three-year sequence. Sue and John take two years, but in different combinations. Carol and Bill each devote virtually full time (4 credits) to the curriculum for one year. This option seems most appropriate for those students seriously interested in citizen action who wish to become immersed in it without being interrupted by other school requirements. The full-year program might be seen as a secondary school equivalent of Peace Corps, VISTA, a year abroad, an honors' thesis, or work experience that allows intensive and sus-

TABLE 3
Citizen action courses taken by five students during the tenth, eleventh, and twelfth grades

Student	Grade 10	Grade 11	Grade 12
Mike	B[a]	A[b]	C[c]
Sue	B	A C	
John		A B	C
Carol		A B C	
Bill			A B C

[a]Winning Support: Persuasion and Group Work, 1 English credit.
[b]Taking a Stand: Moral Deliberation and Social Policy Research, 1 social studies credit.
[c]Practicum in the Exercise of Influence: 1/2 social studies, 1/2 English, and 1 flexible credit.

tained concentration in one area. Ideally, a school would offer the three courses in a way that allowed for this option. There should also be an opportunity for students to choose the more gradual, exploratory route. According to our recommendations, it is possible that at any given time (say, 1977), all five students representing grades ten through twelve would be in the same class, for example, "Winning Support" (B).

Selection of Students

Which students should take this program? Should it be required or elective? Should there be any special admission criteria? Some might assert, for example, that these courses be mandatory for those students least able to exert influence in the society: the exploited and the powerless need such instruction more than those who already wield power and influence. Others might see them as particularly necessary for ruling elites, to help them exert influence more wisely or justly. Yet others might propose the courses for students who wish to become political scientists, on the grounds that experiential learning in the exercise of influence must complement academic study of that subject.

Although we argued in Chapter 2 that the ability to exert influence in public affairs should be considered an educational objective appropriate for all students, actual coursework in this area should not be required for all students or for any special group, for such a requirement at this point would constitute a publicly imposed, but unjustified restriction on students' freedom. To justify such restrictions on individual choice, one must be able to demonstrate with a high degree of certainty that beneficial consequences will ensue from the requirement and, further, that the beneficial consequences can be justified as overriding whatever disadvantages accrue to the individual as a result of the restriction on freedom. Unfortunately, we know very little about how to instruct students in order to increase their ability to exert influence in public affairs. Thus, at this point we cannot point with much certainty to any beneficial outcomes of requiring students to take such instruction. Even if we could "guarantee" increased ability to exert influence as a result of required instruction, it would still be difficult to show that this beneficial result outweighs various disadvantages that might accompany such a requirement (such as depriving a student of the opportunity to study other subjects). Until we gain more knowledge about how to implement this curriculum successfully, courses must remain elective or voluntary.[2]

Although the courses should be chosen voluntarily, it might be necessary to select from among the volunteers. Such selection would be necessary if there were more applicants than could be accommodated by the school's resources, or, even if a school could accommodate all applicants, an argument might be made that some courses would be appropriate only for certain types of students. Because the purpose of this program is to increase ability to exert influence in the political system, the denial of the opportunity to take such courses can be seen as tantamount to restricting political participation. For this reason there is a special burden to justify criteria used to discriminate between "appropriate" and "inappropriate" students. Below we discuss some of the criteria commonly suggested in answer to the question: What qualifications or characteristics should give a student a preferential right to enroll in the courses?

High motivation and some competence to participate. It is argued that students who come to the course with high motivation and some current competence in these matters are more likely to succeed than those uninterested and unskilled. Studies show relatively low levels of citizen participation in public affairs, but, among those who do participate, upper-middle-class students predominate. To use this criterion, then, could merely help the influential and the powerful attain more power and not distribute skills in the exercise of influence more equitably throughout the population. On the other hand, the criterion might lead to better education of the powerful elites, so that they would be more just in their exercise of influence.

Low motivation and low competence. This criterion rests on the concern that the alienated, uninterested, unskilled student needs such a curriculum more than others and that priority ought to be given to those most deficient in this area. The dropouts, the apathetic students, the highly motivated but incompetent, the competent but unmotivated persons deserve a chance to develop a more

---

2. The argument that universal academic requirements, within compulsory public education, are unjustified restrictions on human freedom applies as well to requirements for conventional coursework (e.g., a year of U.S. history). Many existing requirements in schools could not meet the challenge of this position.

effective voice in determining their destiny, but engaging the unengaged student is difficult and certain students may be virtually uneducable in this area. While we must clearly put more effort into reaching the apparently unreachable, it would be difficult to defend restricting instruction to this group alone. Some students would be denied the opportunity to develop their skills further, and resources might be wasted on hopeless cases.

Membership in a powerless group. Regardless of one's level of interest or skill, it might be argued that unrepresented, disenfranchised, exploited, powerless persons deserve first priority in order to combat efforts of the influential and the powerful to deprive such groups of basic rights, goods, services, and the chance to participate. This principle is persuasive, for it aims toward more equitable distribution of power in the society. Yet it is not sufficient. There is serious difficulty in identifying powerless groups and in deciding who is most powerless. Should the course be restricted to blacks, low-income people, consumers, farm laborers, prisoners, the elderly, independent farmers, or all youth? Even if we could agree on identification of the truly powerless, we might find individuals in that group highly motivated and skilled in the exercise of influence. (Would Martin Luther King have needed the course?) There might also be persons unmotivated and unskilled who could not benefit from the course or persons within the group who might work toward public policies that might even further disenfranchise their own group.

Commitment to the most just public policies. Those who fear that students in this curriculum might learn to exert influence unjustly or to direct it toward undesirable policies feel that instruction should be restricted to those students interested in the "right" kinds of public policies. Some educators may have specific political programs they wish to support, for example, a set of policies aimed at more equitable distribution of wealth, stricter controls on industrial pollution, or expanding public health services. If students were to work against such policies, the educator might view this as the school giving license to the undermining of justice itself. Should such students be given lower priority than those working for the "correct" kinds of policies? It is often difficult to defend judgments as to why certain policies are more "just" than others. Acceptance of this criterion would clearly put the school in the role of advocating specific public policies and of denying students educational opportunities based on these positions. This would constitute unjustified discrimination. Further, from a practical point of view, a school could not survive the conflict arising from this approach.

In spite of these difficulties with criteria for selection of students, it should be recognized that, if instruction in a course is highly specialized and if all students are expected to learn that specialization, certain qualifications or prerequisites can be justified. If, for example, a course is intended to conduct opinion surveys in the community, arithmetic might reasonably be required. If a course requires students to spend much of their time working independently without adult supervision, some evidence that applicants can handle this responsibility might reasonably be required. Even in relatively specialized courses, however, prescribing what all students need to know or what characteristics they must have before they can benefit from instruction remains problematic.

When a course is not specialized and is not planned to provide standard instruction to all students, it becomes even more difficult to establish prerequisites that distinguish qualified from unqualified students. In the Madison course we wished to encourage a variety of activities and learnings, depending upon individual interests, and, therefore, it was virtually impossible to set criteria that would fairly select some students over others. Ideally, one might hope to diagnose students sufficiently to predict how much each applicant would benefit or grow as a result of instruction in a forthcoming course. Lacking the knowledge to make reliable predictions on these matters, however, we chose to open the course to any volunteers, grades nine through twelve. It was decided that a lottery would be used to limit enrollment if necessary.

Although the course was open to any student, we hoped that each applicant would be seriously committed to becoming involved in a community action project. A great variety of students enrolled: some wanted field trips; some wanted an unstructured class allowing them to rap with peers; some wanted to explore vocations. Only a few matched our original image of a potential student activist. Our "welcome-with-open-arms" admission policy had been interpreted as an opportunity to "do your own thing." Confronted with this diverse group, the staff had to decide whether all students should be required to take action on public issues or whether they should be free to work on whatever questions, projects, or concerns might interest them. Some staff members favored a restrictive focus on social action, but realized that the course description and previous recruiting messages had not emphasized this sufficiently to impose it. The decision was to allow a wide spectrum of community involvement.

A broad conception of community involvement (volunteer work, social research, advocacy, exploratory sojourns into the community) creates no problem in student selection, for, by definition, one tries to meet all individual needs. Even with a narrower focus, however, it remains almost impossible to justify standards based on students' knowledge, skills, motivation, character traits, social class, membership, or any other factor. One can, however, use *student self-selection* to attain some selectivity without imposing arbitrary qualifications. If a narrowly conceived course can be justified (for example, a course focusing totally on exerting influence on a local zoning board dealing with environmental issues), it should be clearly advertised as such. The rules, requirements, and procedures should be publicized well enough so that appropriate students are encouraged to apply and inappropriate ones are discouraged. Recruitment efforts should attempt to make such a course equally attractive to all students, including special efforts to reach the otherwise unreachable, but it is not necessary to teach a course that meets all needs of all students. Although we did not pursue this approach vigorously enough, powerful dissemination techniques could justifiably be used to create expectations that would attract to the course primarily the type of student desired. This gives no assurance that only the right students will apply, and staff must be prepared for students who seek experiences quite different from the official purpose of the course.

The self-imposed selectivity seems to represent the most reasonable method of selection. Here the significance of the main objective —increased ability to exert influence in public affairs—should be strongly publicized. This must be translated into terms meaningful to a wide variety of students by giving numerous examples of the kinds of activities that could be pursued (along with contrasting examples of those which seem to fall beyond the boundaries) and the ways in which the knowledge, skills, and attitudes that lie at the heart of the curriculum might be important in students' lives. Faculty expectations—the amount of work required, methods of evaluation, and so forth—should be made clear, but they should not be meant to discourage less able students. Efforts should be made to prevent the program from becoming a "dumping ground," but the presence of uncommitted students in a course is an inevitable result of voluntary student selection. This is a risk that must be taken. No doubt it is a challenge to faculty morale, but it must not be allowed to change the central objective of instruction.

Administration-Management

A program that sends many groups of students to different parts of the community to work under the supervision of "uncertified" adults, is obviously more complicated to manage than a conventional course in a self-contained classroom. While there are no recipes for successful program administration, certain major issues can be clarified.

Facilities

A well-equipped citizen action laboratory is more expensive than a conventional classroom. It requires access to a variety of equipment: telephones, mimeograph and photocopy machines, cameras, tape recorders, equipment for making signs and posters, loudspeakers, filing cabinets, typewriters, televisions, radios. Materials such as stationery and stamps, mailing lists, specialized directories, maps, selected legal references, periodicals, and newspapers should be available. Students also need rooms for small and large group meetings and space for storing project-related material.

This is not to suggest that all such facilities be located at one place or reserved only for students in the citizen action program. To provide all conceivably useful supplies could in fact violate a central message of the curriculum: to meet one's needs and secure one's rights, one should and can exert influence upon the environment. To practice what it preaches, a citizen action program must require students to act on their own initiative to obtain some facilities, but this approach should not be taken to the extreme of providing only a roof and four bare walls. The staff, realizing that students may need many of these items, should meet minimal requirements and cooperate in helping students secure other items either within the school or outside. To the extent that such facilities are available only outside of the school, students should be expected (and even encouraged) to work where the facilities are available rather than in school.

Liability

School-sponsored activity outside of school raises questions about the supervisory responsibilities and legal duties of teachers and other adults with whom students come in contact. Suppose a student is injured in an off-campus community activity. Who can be held liable for damages? The answer is complicated and depends upon a number of conditions. Part of the ambiguity is due to the absence of a well-developed body of school law based on court opinions stemming from actual cases dealing with school-sponsored community involvement. There is, of course, a considerable body of law concerning the general question of liability related to personal injury (torts). A review of this field provides three principles that help to prevent a teacher or a school administration from being held liable for injuries that might befall a student in the course of citizen action projects.[3]

First, parents and students should be fully informed as to possible risks associated with such instruction. Before the course begins, general information should be distributed on the range of activities, their location, the type of adult supervision provided (including illustrations of situations in which no adult supervision can be guaranteed), provisions for transportation of students (or lack thereof), and so forth. Once the course has begun, the teacher should be continuously informed as to the students' activities and should make this information available to parents periodically so that they have more specific information on possible risks to their child. The school, in other words, has an obligation to make "full disclosure" regarding conditions of the course that may affect the safety of each child.

Second, parents and students should give written consent to participate in the course under the conditions that have been disclosed. The school should design a form for this purpose. Note that consent could be given to a number of different conditions. Some parents may consent to virtually no adult supervision at any time for their child. Others may request that adults supervise transportation, but only that. Still others may want the presence of a certified teacher at all times before giving consent to a community involvement program. Some may be satisfied if they are simply informed by the school as

---

3. I am grateful to David J. Hanson, University of Wisconsin, for consulting on legal aspects of this problem. This analysis should not be taken as legal advice but as general information that should be supplemented by views of local officials and attorneys.

to their child's destination on each trip away from school. Depending upon parents' feelings in a specific community, the teacher and school can design a written consent form that makes it possible for parents to make clear the "risks" to which they give consent. The range of options will of necessity be limited by what is considered administratively feasible by the teacher and the school administration. To fully comply with this principle of "informed consent," a course that involves any risks beyond those normally associated with school attendance would have to be voluntary, that is, an elective and not a required course.

Finally, the school teacher and any other adults charged with supervisory responsibility for students must not act negligently and must take reasonable actions to prevent harm to the student. This duty is not susceptible to precise definition. Its definition depends for content on a case-by-case analysis related to particular facts. It is referred to in the law as what can be rightfully expected of the "prudent and reasonable man." Extreme examples can illustrate, but in no way comprehensively define, this duty. One would not begin an auto trip in a blinding snowstorm against police warnings of hazardous driving conditions. If a local riot is announced, one would not take students into the heat of the action in order to experience social conflict firsthand.

This third principle involves not simply the doctrine of the prudent and reasonable man, but also the state's obligation (in its public educational system) to look after the welfare of the child. This may in certain situations require the teacher to act assertively to keep students out of trouble. If students engage in potentially dangerous or unlawful activity and injury does result, the teacher may have to demonstrate not only that he or she vigorously warned students against it, but that as much action as could be reasonably expected was taken to prevent it.

By raising the liability problem and treating it cautiously from a legal standpoint, we do not wish to elevate its significance. It is true that many teachers, administrators, and parents may see this as a serious issue, but fortunately their concern is often unnecessary. The accident rate in school-related activities is extremely low, and school activities in other areas—shop, home economics, athletics—are more dangerous than community involvement. We must also remember that a person or institution can be held liable for injuries *only if it is demonstrated that they acted negligently.* Finally, even if a person is found negligent, there is liability insurance, and damages are not likely to exceed the amount of insured coverage.

School teachers or other adults with supervisory responsibilities in a community involvement program should ascertain the extent of their insured liability coverage. The teacher is usually protected under a school policy. One should clarify, however, whether the school policy applies to the type of community involvement in question. If students are transported by private auto, one should also clarify that type of coverage. The school might agree to assume liability beyond a teacher's personal coverage up to a certain amount, and it might make a similar arrangement for other adults participating in the program. Adults teaching students in their workplaces should also clarify the extent of their liability insurance. I am aware of no nation-wide study on insurance protection for this type of course, but neither have I encountered any instance where proper protection could not be provided. Nor am I aware of any unreasonable increases in costs to teachers or other adults for such protection.

Relations with the Community

A citizen action program will become known to adults who have only incidental contact with the program (a shopper interviewed by a student); those who have agreed to be available to work with the program (a lawyer who volunteers to help students, should they be interested); and those who actually do work with students in the program (a city planner who supervises two student interns twice a week). Members of the general public may begin to question why the students are not in school "where they belong." To help satisfy curiosity or defuse the alarm of the general public, students and teachers should be able to offer a coherent explanation of the rationale, objectives, and procedures of the program. A brochure containing this information should be readily available for distribution.

When a resource file of agencies and individuals willing to cooperate with the program is being compiled, it is often necessary to seek tentative and ambiguous commitments from potential adult volunteers. In the Madison program where students had complete freedom to choose the projects and adults with whom they would work, we could not promise any adult volunteer that he or she would in fact be selected. The purpose of the list is to determine which people would be available in case students did wish to work with them. Potential volunteers often need to know how much time will be required and when their services might be needed. They may want to know specifics of their supervisory responsibilities, and they may require that students make definite time commitments before they offer their services. If a potential volunteer specifies conditions under which he or she can offer help to students, this information should be included in the resource file. Uncertainty can be further reduced if students are limited in their choice of projects. Particular projects and internships could be established in advance of a course, and students assigned to them. Such assignments could be publicized prior to registration so that only those students willing to accept specific placement would be eligible for the course.

As students begin to explore resources and projects, it is important to coordinate inquiries directed toward a given person or agency. Having to respond to fourteen different students asking the same questions on fourteen different occasions is an unnecessary inconvenience for prospective community teachers, and this can be avoided by arranging for coordinated visits. Coordination of this sort requires that students have access to information on the destination, dates, times, and purposes of their colleagues' inquiry into community agencies, and that certain visits be scheduled to avoid conflict. Information gained from a visit can be provided to those students who were unable to attend.

Adults who work with students on a continuous basis may desire consultation with the school teacher, the student, or the student's parents. Is the community teacher making a contribution to the student's education? Has the student been evaluated fairly? How could clashes of personality or ideology between student and community teacher be handled more constructively? What could the school teacher do in school to make the community involvement experience more productive? Community teachers could benefit from sharing experiences among themselves on how they relate to the students, as students could benefit from comparing notes on their relationships with separate community teachers. Such meetings can reflect varying degrees of formality, from chats over coffee to picnics to conferences to seminars. The major challenge for the school teacher is to keep communication open among the various parties connected to the course. This helps not only to relieve a sense of isolation on the part of individual students and community teachers, but also to develop a public identity for the course and a forum for helping community teachers assess their educational contribution.[4]

Students are often eager to have their work publicly recognized through the press, TV, and radio, and much can be learned about the media itself by becoming its subject. The staff must develop policies for handling such publicity. Should the teacher review all news that students wish to give to the press? Should the teacher accept responsibility for responding to public reaction to the press? To what extent should other school authorities become involved? Publicity on students' projects dramatically calls attention to a course in citizen action. It thereby becomes a more public form of education (in the sense of having greater public exposure) than that offered in the confines of a classroom. This creates not only the problem of devising an approach to public relations that assists rather than harms the course, but also challenges the teacher to determine the extent to which he or she is willing to expose the course to the type of public scrutiny that can easily be avoided in a conventional classroom.

Certain problems in community relations may be minimized if the citizen action curriculum is endorsed by a citizens' advisory committee consisting of parents, students, teachers, and a few community leaders. Without running the daily affairs of the program, a committee could advise on general policy, suggest resources, and lend a broad base of support. This can be crucial to a teaching staff that, in times of controversy, may need special help, but would otherwise be isolated. A smoothly functioning committee can contribute to program visibility, security, and also creativity in the curriculum itself.

Relations within the School

A citizen action course may be considered unique in a school, strikingly different from other courses. Staff and students may feel that students enrolled in the course have special privileges: more mobility within and outside school; the use of phones, mimeograph machines, bulletin boards, media, and other facilities not commonly

---

4. There is wide agreement that volunteer workers benefit from contact with each other in "support groups" where they can establish some distance from their individual volunteer responsibilities and can compare experiences. Similarly, community teachers might benefit from sharing their experiences in situations that allow them to remove themselves from their commitment to a specific young person or job.

used in regular courses; more guest speakers or members of the community coming to the school; less traditional homework assignments and examinations; in general, more independence and less adult supervision. The Madison course did differ in these ways from regular courses, and, as an apparent result, students within the course even began to view themselves as a privileged elite. This can create serious tensions within the school. In the minds of many staff and students, it may seem totally unwise or unjust to bestow such privileges on one group while denying them to others. Participants in such courses must guard against arrogant, elitist behavior. Excessive talking in the halls, clowning while waiting for transportation, or monopolizing bulletin boards and public announcement systems can irritate the larger school community. Teachers must then answer to their colleagues for the disruptive conduct of the students.

Even more demanding to a teacher is the challenge to demonstrate the academic legitimacy of "action," for some critics will judge the course to have no substance or "discipline." Chapters 1 and 2 of this book have, I hope, established the potential educational value of citizen action curriculum. In addition, critiques of common conceptions of "disciplined" learning (for example, Newmann, 1967; Lamm, 1972) can be invoked to show the difficulties of basing curriculum only upon a notion of "solid content." In the face of questions about special privileges for students, the course in question must prove to the school community not only that students can exercise special privileges without disturbing others, but that these conditions are necessary to pursue a valid form of education.

A citizen action course can also be plagued by the "dumping ground" or catchall syndrome. Because it is seen as unique, both staff and students may regard such a course as a panacea for a host of educational ills. Guidance counselors or advisers, when confronted with students who despise all of the conventional course offerings, may recommend a community involvement course as something refreshing, a change of pace. Students alienated by lack of relevance or the oppressive structure of many courses elect the community involvement course as an escape from the system. Administrators recommend the course to "get the activists and troublemakers off our backs." Parents wish to prevent their children from dropping out of school so they recommend this course as a last resort. Any course expected to meet such needs is doomed to failure. To avoid becoming a catchall course, the staff must make a special effort to communicate to the entire school exactly what such a course will and will not attempt to accomplish and whom it intends to serve.

Instructional Climate

Any institutionalized program carries with it significant messages, sometimes explicit, sometimes hidden, about the real reasons for its existence. The ways in which participants interpret these messages dramatically affects their participation. Will students view citizen action courses simply as another arena for gamesmanship in making it through their term in the school "prison"? Will they view such courses as novel ways for adults to foist upon children notions of the "right" preparation required to become a productive citizen? Will the courses, in spite of rhetoric about helping them exert influence, actually inhibit their use of power? Although the curriculum may officially stress the importance of collective cooperation in the exercise of influence, does instruction encourage destructive individual competition? The discussion has not yet consolidated our observations on how various programming devices can suppress or nurture the essential spirit of a citizen action curriculum. A few ways in which conventional approaches may violate the spirit of our curriculum model, as well as some alternatives that might correct this, follow.

Area 1. Paternalism versus self-assertion. In several ways a school can convey the idea that prepackaged education has been prepared by adults who know what is best and that the student role is to receive and absorb it, passively accepting what is given in their environment. This message is manifested, however unintentionally, when the teacher programs in advance, without student input, everything that a student will do in a course (readings, assignments, exercises, games, exams, field trips); when the school provides for the student all the resources needed for learning; when the school establishes for students a system of governance that allows them no responsibility for the making or enforcing of policy and insists that they obey policies made by adults; when particular school policies actually *prohibit* students from exerting influence in their environment (no decoration of the walls, no student participation in school landscaping, no use of school facilities for conduct of political campaigns). For citizen action curriculum to be consistent with its philosophy, it must avoid these practices.

Social action courses should place students in roles where they assume meaningful responsibility for asserting themselves. Instead of being engaged in learning with only private consequences, students working toward adoption or repeal of actual policies will be publicly accountable for some of their actions. This can be particularly important in the school environment where students have a voice, though not a unilateral one, in determining their own citizen action curriculum. As mentioned earlier, students should have to act assertively to acquire resources, apart from minimal ones (especially telephones) that must be supplied at the outset. In the action project method discussed in Chapter 5, students will be involved in the formulation of their own learning objectives and the content of the course as the project unfolds; it is virtually impossible for a teacher to structure their learning in any detail prior to the onset of a project. Within a single course and operating within the larger school structure, students may, in concert with the teacher, establish policies on attendance, evaluation, requirements for "products," methods for access to facilities. More extensive opportunities for governance could be provided by the "sabbatical" model, a one-year, full-time curriculum in which students earn all four credits related to citizen action. Under this program students would have no major obligations to other courses within the school, and they could, therefore, participate in authentic governance of their own separate program.

In general, the exercise of influence as a central purpose of curriculum stands opposed to paternalistic climates and to apathetic or fatalistic orientations. ("Accept the world as it is, for there is nothing we can do to change it.") Instead, self-assertion to affect the environment is valued. When students encounter obstacles to self-assertion in the school itself (a rule against painting the walls, or lack of student representation on the school board), they must be encouraged to investigate the justifications behind apparent obstacles. They must not be penalized for mounting campaigns against them. A citizen action curriculum will be ineffective unless the general school climate supports self-assertion—making an impact in the immediate environment as well as in the community beyond the school.

Area 2. Individualism versus collective cooperation. The ensuing critique of individualism should be seen in light of the fact that the curriculum proposed here rests on the basic ethical obligation to respect the dignity of each individual human. To secure one's rights in public affairs, however, it becomes necessary for the individual to work within collectives of persons with mutual interests. Many facets of school, through overwhelming attention to the individual, communicate a conspicuous lack of recognition of the significance of collective effort and responsibility. While we often complain that instruction in the school is not individualized enough, a climate of preoccupation with the individual to the exclusion of the collective is illustrated in many practices.

Programs of instruction are selected for students based, presumably, on individualized counseling and career planning, giving students the impression that the entire purpose of education is to enhance one's individual mobility or opportunity in life. Learning materials are assigned to individual students (checking out of library books or equipment), and locker space is also allocated on an individual basis. Discipline is oriented toward finding the individual responsible for breaking the rules. Work assignments within courses are the responsibility of individual students. Cooperation with others in the completion of work is often harshly punished as "cheating." Finally, the grading system assigns marks to individuals and encourages competitive individual comparison by bestowing status upon high rank in class. Awards to valedictorians and special privileges for other high academic achievers further reinforces individual competition.

This is not to say that all such practices should be abolished, for instructional programs must recognize individual needs and must also hold individuals responsible for their actions. Citizen action curriculum, however, faces a special challenge to convey to students the significance and legitimacy of collective action and cooperation. Because of a dominant emphasis on individualism in our society, the collective mentality may be difficult to establish, but we can suggest some practices to assist in this effort. In citizen action courses, individual students should not be allowed to go off and do their individual "thing," for their ability to exert influence in public policy will not be enhanced unless they learn to work within groups. Student work should be organized into group activities, and various members involved in a project should all have responsibilities that assist in reaching a common goal. The evaluation of student performance can similarly be oriented toward accomplishments and shortcomings of the group rather than the comparative achievements of individuals. All individual evaluation should not, however, be abandoned. Individuals within groups should evaluate each other as to the extent of their contribution to the group effort and how that contribution might be enhanced in the future. Responsibility for equipment and for obedience to institutional policy can also be assigned to a project group, with the group as a whole being responsible for losses or infractions. Internally, the group could distribute blame or punishment as it deemed just. The point of modifying instructional climate in such ways is not to stamp out individualism, but to prevent its excesses from inhibiting the collective effort required in the exercise of influence.

Area 3. Intrinsic versus extrinsic value. Much activity in school, if valued at all by students, is valued only for its extrinsic or instrumental worth. Studying X is good because it leads to something else, such as a diploma, a college education, or money. The instrumental nature of human activity pervades the instructional climate as teachers candidly inform students that they may not enjoy X, but it is necessary if they wish to move ahead in life. Many educators cannot justify, either to themselves or to students, certain aspects of the curriculum except that they are required by some other institution.

The fragmentation of time in scheduling reflects in part the primacy of extrinsic over intrinsic values. If, in a student's eyes, a subject is worthy of study in its own right, there is no reason why the ringing of a bell or the requirement that one must also complete work in other subjects simultaneously should prevent the student from pursuing it. A busy schedule can make it virtually impossible to become absorbed in something intrinsically satisfying, and students have little choice but to roam through the curriculum touching many subjects superficially.

Citizen action courses must take care not to communicate to students the idea that instruction in this area is merely a vehicle to some other value (good citizenship or personal power). Avoiding this message may be difficult, for our own curriculum conception does posit social action activity as one means toward the end of exerting influence. At the same time, we do recognize that, if students are led to construe their work *only* as means, lacking intrinsic value, they are unlikely to become seriously engaged. An instructional climate might emphasize the intrinsic worth of an activity if students are allowed to pursue it in a sustained fashion, uninterrupted by other obligations; if staff members show enthusiasm for its intrinsic value and can rationally justify its value in other than instrumental terms; and if formal institutional rewards and punishments for engaging in the activity or for one's level of performance therein are kept to a minimum. These recommendations on instructional climate would, of course, be appropriate to curriculum in general, not limited to the objective of increasing student effectiveness in public affairs.

Conclusion

While these various program recommendations may seem to entail large-scale innovation, they do constitute a compromise. Proposals for curriculum change are often either too miniscule or too grandiose. That is, many limit their scope to revision of existing single courses on the assumption that these can be most easily adapted to the present structure. Unfortunately, the overwhelming influence of the general structure of school often nullifies the impact of exciting reforms in single courses. At the other extreme are those proposals for nothing less than a total overhauling of the secondary curriculum. Some of these efforts are successful in small alternative schools, but fundamental alteration of the comprehensive high school is virtually impossible. A middle-ground approach is to establish multicredit programs within the existing curriculum, occupying enough of the students' time so as to have a significant impact but not trying to replace completely the existing curriculum. This strategy allows students to take advantage of beneficial aspects of the present structure, but it also allows them the opportunity to participate in a program with a separate identity and special spirit. The approach also responds to the professional concerns of teachers, for there are groups of teachers in many schools who wish to experiment with innovations not accepted by the faculty-at-large. Multicredit programs provide these teachers with an opportunity to work together and to influence students without necessarily having to convert the entire faculty. Such a strategy is consistent with the "school-within-a-school" concept and the growing effort to design pluralistic alternative programs within the secondary curriculum.

CHAPTER 5
Choices in Teaching

Some issues in program design were discussed in Chapter 4; now it is appropriate to examine issues involved in the design of instruction. This chapter outlines a number of choices available to teachers who must confront the problems involved with organizing instruction, facilitating student projects, functioning in alternative teacher roles, and evaluating action learning. This discussion, again based on the Madison experience, raises issues that might not otherwise have been anticipated and offers some recommendations.

Organization of Instruction

In planning specific learning experiences to meet objectives of the citizen action agenda, important, but often unrecognized, choices can establish an underlying structure for instruction. Choices discussed here are not unique to citizen action curriculum; they are common to all curriculum planning. These decisions are usually made only indirectly or implicitly, but, because they have considerable impact in the learning environment, educators should face them directly at initial stages in the design of a course or a general curriculum.

Objectives

The general objective of increasing student ability to exert influence in public affairs can be reduced to somewhat more specific objectives, as was done in Chapter 3. The next question is: Which, if any, of these objectives should all students master at some minimal level of competence? Some students may be interested only in organization-administration-management; others, only in group process; and still others, in none of the action competencies. The course in Madison gave the impression that students could use it to meet a variety of individual needs, and the staff, therefore, did not require all students to achieve any single objective. In the curriculum suggested earlier (Chapter 4), there could be some objectives within each course that all students might be required to achieve at some minimal level, but others would be optional. The decision as to which instructional objectives should be applied homogeneously to all students and which should be unique or idiosyncratic to individual students establishes one dimension of an underlying structure. Whether a specific course or an entire curriculum is being organized, decisions on the question of homogeneity versus heterogeneity of objectives can be viewed on a continuum:

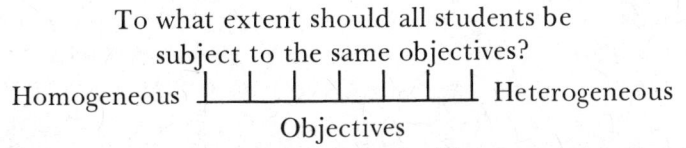

To what extent should all students be
subject to the same objectives?

Homogeneous |⎯|⎯|⎯|⎯|⎯|⎯| Heterogeneous
Objectives

The extreme case of homogeneity of objectives is a situation in which all students are required to learn identical bits of knowledge, skills, and attitudes, and these constitute the *only* objectives of the curriculum. The extreme case of heterogeneity is a situation in which *any* objective that any student might have would be considered a legitimate basis for the curriculum.[1]

Methods

A second choice concerns the extent to which all students ought to learn according to the same method, regardless of objectives. Even if students differed in their objectives, it is conceivable that all might be required to learn through the same methods or experiences. All might

---

1. By heterogeneity of objectives, we mean that different students will be allowed to have different objectives. Several students might happen to have a single objective in common; for example, mastery of techniques in political canvassing. Other students might aim toward skills in physical therapy for the mentally retarded. Heterogeneity of objectives should not be confused with multiple objectives. One cannot have heterogeneity of objectives in a group of students without multiple objectives; one can, however, have multiple objectives without having heterogeneity. A teacher who requires that all students master three specific objectives has a set of multiple objectives that are applied homogeneously to all students.

be engaged in volunteer work, all might keep a diary, or all might attend certain class discussions. Or, even if a standard objective were prescribed for all students—for example, skills in social policy research—different learning methods might be proposed for different students. Some might work primarily with published documents, some might conduct interviews or canvasses, and others might serve as interns with policy makers. The examples indicate that homogeneity or heterogeneity in objectives of instruction does not necessarily require the same policy for methods of instruction, and vice versa. In the Madison course we chose, in a very broad sense, a single method for all students: "a community involvement project." Each student was required to join with at least one other student to define and execute some project. Students were also required to meet often with adult staff members to discuss their work and to report on their projects orally and in writing to the rest of the class. Because the nature of the projects varied considerably, however, one might question whether this actually constituted a single method for all.

The agenda for citizen action curriculum contains no detailed recommendations on methods, although the conduct of student projects is discussed later. Because of students' sensitive resistance to being programmed into standardized packages and because of individual differences in styles of learning, it seems important to create an instructional structure that allows for considerable heterogeneity in learning experiences. Curricular decisions on methods can also be located on a scale:

To what extent should all students learn through the same methods (experiences)?

Homogeneous |__|__|__|__|__|__| Heterogeneous
Methods

Conclusions here would depend upon the level of abstraction at which methods or experiences are construed. We might require that all students have an experience in advocacy, persuading another individual to lend support. Described at this level of generality, it suggests a homogeneous policy. If, however, students were allowed to select a diverse set of causes and diverse audiences to persuade, the instructional experiences would reflect a more heterogeneous pattern.

Control

Whether learning experiences be similar for all or different for each student, another feature in the organization of instruction is the extent of deliberate control exercised over learning activities. Where there is a high degree of control, learning experiences are systematically planned, and one can predict which activities precede and follow others. Where there is a low degree of control, learning experiences occur in an unpredictable sequence, apparently more in response to unforeseen needs of the moment than to some predetermined plan. At one extreme, a teacher could exert great control by providing a selected set of readings, a series of lectures, a set of hand-picked adult community consultants to visit the class, and a semester-long program of class activities. At the other extreme, a teacher could avoid all such devices and simply instruct students to venture into the community to learn something meaningful about, say, problems of research on social policy. In most situations decisions on the degree of control are essentially decisions about how much control the teacher should exert, but degree of control should be seen as an independent dimension distinct from the source of control or the locus of authority. Even if students were given total authority over a class, they would still have to decide how much control to exert. *Who* should exert control is another matter.

Decisions on degree of control can be independent of decisions on homogeneity versus heterogeneity in objectives or in learning experiences. A course where students use programmed instruction to work at their own pace on a variety of objectives represents a highly controlled learning experience, yet there are different objectives for each student. In contrast, a teacher might support a variety of learning methods for different students (reading, field trips, internships, action projects, volunteer service), yet impose a high degree of control on the individualized method (an explicit written contract, frequent reports, teacher-selected community projects). Finally, there can be a homogeneous method, such as visiting the legislature, with a low degree of control if, for example, the teacher exerted no influence in the planning, execution, or evaluation of the visit. In the Madison course relatively little control was exerted on the class as a whole, but individual staff members had the authority to exert the amount of control they deemed appropriate on a given group at a given point in time. In general, the control imposed was mainly procedural—making sure that students had some plan, that they had considered a variety of alternatives, that they avoided disastrous mistakes.

Degree of control within a course can be assessed with reference to a third scale:

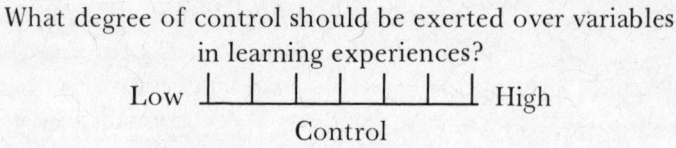

What degree of control should be exerted over variables
in learning experiences?

Low └─┴─┴─┴─┴─┴─┘ High

Control

To the extent that adolescents want liberation from arbitrary, unreasonable forms of adult-imposed control in their lives, they may react against any form of control or systematic planning. "Hanging loose," "playing it cool," or other similar attributes admired in the peer culture, while they signify a sense of inner *self*-control, can be viewed as reactions against the formal organization of experience into predictable components. Even when students are given the power to exert significant control, as in the governance of alternative schools, many prefer a spontaneous, ad hoc, flexible approach.

Authority

To reach and defend conclusions on these three aspects in the organization of instruction is difficult, but an even more fundamental choice remains: Which authority or combination of authorities (staff, students, parents) ought to have final say in deciding objectives that should be pursued, methods of learning that should be included, and how much control should be exerted in the learning situation? In the Madison course, adult staff were the ultimate authority on each of these issues, and their decisions tended toward heterogeneity of objectives, heterogeneity of specific learning experiences, and low degree of control. In effect, these decisions delegated major responsibility to students. To the extent that staff retains legal responsibility for the planning and teaching of curriculum, the authority question may seem academic, for such authority can ultimately be transferred elsewhere only if this is permitted by a benevolent staff. Even then, permission can always be rescinded.

Because adolescents, like humans in general, often have deep emotional investments in questions of authority, the nature of authority relationships is a powerful force within a learning environment. We cannot recommend an authority structure appropriate for all citizen action curricula, but each curriculum should take pains to convey accurate information about the authority structure that does prevail. Faculty who appear liberal in allowing students considerable freedom in the selection of topics may have rigorous, possibly narrow, standards for evaluating student performance. The student who receives a low grade may charge the teacher with hypocrisy: "You were nice in allowing us the freedom to do our thing, and now you flunk me because I didn't play the game your way." By equating the right to select a topic of study with the right to set standards for adequate performance, the student came to perceive an inconsistency in the authority structure. Open discussion about the actual authority structure within a course might help to avoid such confusion. The salience of this problem, especially in courses construed as different from "school as usual," demands that it be given more explicit attention in curriculum planning.

Student Projects

For each component in the model, our curriculum assumes some student involvement in the community. While the most ambitious projects would occur in the practicum, instruction in the two single courses should also provide project opportunities. The importance of community involvement projects requires some discussion of their implementation.

Types

There are at least three types of community involvement, but they are not mutually exclusive.[2] In *exploratory research,* students investigate the community, gathering information through field trips, interviews, guest speakers, informal observation in community institutions, and other means. Such research can be superficial and transient, as when students try to get a "taste" or "sense" of community life by following their curiosity from architect to landlord to shopkeeper to politician. Students can also make intensive studies of particular issues, however, collecting and organizing information in ways that provide information useful not only to themselves but also to the community-at-large.

Volunteer service, a second form of involvement, often places students in a direct helping relationship to other individuals. Student placements in a home for the elderly, a day-care center, a tutoring

---

2. In its taxonomy of roles for youth that go beyond community involvement, the National Commission on Resources for Youth (1974) has identified projects for youth as curriculum builders, teachers, community manpower, entrepreneurs, community problem solvers, communicators, and resources for youth.

program, a neighborhood cleanup campaign, or a survey of lead poisoning in young children are examples of a growing volunteer movement that found initial federal support at the college level (Peace Corp and VISTA) but is being increasingly sponsored by high schools.[3] Volunteer service in helping relationships can develop environmental competence, and it usually involves more long-term commitment and responsibility to others than exploratory research projects. Volunteer projects, however, do not often attempt to wield influence upon public policy, and, while they may assist in the learning of citizen action skills, they should not be considered synonymous with social action.

Social action projects may depend heavily upon information gathered through community research activity and may be stimulated by injustices observed as a result of volunteer service. But in requiring the student to take a stand that must be advocated, social action projects differ from the first two forms of community involvement. Becoming a persuader, advocate, or organizer may seem psychologically more risky than becoming a gatherer of information or a volunteer helper and, as outlined in our agenda, the successful exercise of influence may demand complicated skills. Of the three types, social action projects relate most directly to the central goal of increasing student ability to exert influence, but exploratory research and volunteer service projects can certainly facilitate the attainment of citizen action competencies.

Psychological and socialization theory leads to a speculation that the three types of projects might nurture successive stages in growth from child to adult that have been described in terms of movement from egocentrism to sociocentrism and from dependence to independence. During exploratory research the students remain relatively self-oriented, trying to gather information interesting to themselves, but, nevertheless, venturing beyond a protected environment into the community. During volunteer service the students extend themselves further to care for or help others in a way that need not be highly threatening, but that does provide the adult sense of being needed by others. Finally, in the advocacy role, students emerge as more auton-

---

3. For information on the volunteer service movement at the secondary level, consult organizations listed in the Appendix, especially the following publications of ACTION, National Student Volunteer Program: *High School Student Volunteers; High School Courses with Volunteer Components*; and the *Synergist,* 2:2, Fall 1973.

omous, independent agents with concerns and efforts that go beyond service to individuals and extend to institutions in the community-at-large.

Students will want to know what constitutes a "legitimate" type of project. The course in Madison, while it encouraged students to select social action projects, allowed all three types, and we found students to be interested in a diverse range, only a few of which could be considered pure advocacy or social action efforts. Related to our discussion on organization of instruction, staff must be prepared to indicate what kinds of projects, if any, will not be allowed. In spite of our endorsement of heterogeneous learning experiences, we would probably not, for example, have permitted such projects as review of science fiction novels, a school dance, or rebuilding cars.

Project Selection: The Orientation Problem

If students ought to have a choice in the selection of projects, how can instruction assist them in choosing? Presumably, an orientation on alternative possibilities, including field trips, guest speakers, and a list of people and organizations willing to work with students would be desirable. Much class time could be spent examining a "menu." While such an orientation is helpful for some students, for others it can be counterproductive. If compulsory for all, a long orientation deters some students from active involvement in projects to which they are already committed. And, for the ambivalent student, such a "smorgasbord" style of orientation can create even more indecision.

The very act of presenting a wide variety of possibilities, each receiving "equal time," may convey a sense that no single issue need be taken very seriously, thereby increasing student interest in the superficial exploration of many possibilities rather than an in-depth commitment to one. This problem leaves us with "students in search of a cause." In the Madison course, for example, it became all too clear that, even though they voluntarily chose a community issue program, many students felt virtually no self-interest or personal stake in options presented during orientation or even in projects they eventually chose. While they apparently enjoyed their work, many seemed detached from it, viewing it as just another requirement standing in the way of the diploma. This leads us to wonder whether many upper-middle-class, relatively affluent students are too alienated from formal education to become passionately engaged in any projects associated with school. Lack of engagement can be demoralizing to students themselves as they gain awareness of their lack of a personal stake in any project. The realization that a project was selected mainly to fulfill a requirement, or because it seemed more fun or easier than another one, but not for its social significance or intrinsic value may create feelings of guilt, embarrassment, and hypocrisy. There is no panacea for this problem, but discussing it explicitly among staff and students seems necessary. This has a special place in our curriculum under "Personal Motives and Social Justifications."

Orientation seems entirely necessary to inform students of ground rules, protocol in dealing with community agencies, and availability of helpful resources. When orientation is used to present to students multiple options for projects, however, the staff must be alerted to ways in which increased familiarity with alternatives can exacerbate, as well as resolve, student ambivalence and apathy.

Creation of "Products"

Another issue for project-oriented coursework is the definition of the "product" expected to emerge from a project. What, if anything, of a tangible nature should students submit at the conclusion of the project, and to whom (teacher, fellow students, adults in the community)? The question relates to evaluation, which is discussed in more detail later, but it also bears on a conception of instruction inherent in the project method. In this area we recommend that projects should yield preservable products—tape recordings, films, physical models, printed material, or combinations of such media—that can be stored and examined by others. The product should also convey some narrative (if not explicitly, at least through inference) of what the students did during the project. Finally, it should show how students have reflected upon or analyzed the project experience. Examples of possible products that might emerge from different projects are given below:

Projects	Products
Volunteer work in a home for the mentally retarded.	Student diary, including comments about her feelings toward the work and some analysis of differences in personalities among her patients.

Organization of lecture series on environmental problems.	Printed program of the series; photos of speakers and audience; tape recordings or transcripts of lectures.
Campaign to work for a student bill of rights.	Minutes or summaries of meetings with students and adults in the project. Particulars and justification for the rights that have been proposed. Short essay or taped discussion on "what we learned from this project."

The creation of products requires students to reflect about their project, which leads them to conceptualize their work; they do more than merely "have an experience." Such reflection must be accepted as a primary mission of formal education. Guided reflection upon and systematic inquiry into the meaning of experience is the crucial condition that differentiates education for citizen action from citizen action itself. Reflection or inquiry cannot be adequately pursued unless people submit their claims, assertions, interpretations, and ideas to some public scrutiny. Without packaging one's ideas in some presentable fashion, public attention is difficult if not impossible to obtain. Students need not broadcast their innermost thoughts, their private and personal feelings to the public-at-large; violations of privacy cannot necessarily be justified in the name of inquiry or the search for truth. We can acknowledge, however, an obligation to share what one has learned, especially with regard to public affairs, and the creation of products makes this possible.

Group Work and Sharing

Another vehicle to facilitate public testing of one's ideas is to have students work in groups rather than as isolated individuals, making reports to the whole class or to the several groups. On the one hand, staff in the Madison course wished to respect individuality and not to coerce students into sharing responsibility with others. On the other hand, we justified requirements for group work on the grounds that this is necessary for the public pursuit of inquiry; that, to exert influence in public affairs, one must learn to work within groups and one must learn to respond to a public test of one's proposals; and that, because students in a class are part of a collective that may itself be held publicly accountable for its actions, each student has a right to know what classmates are doing. Although the teacher or school superintendent may be legally responsible for the actions of a class, students are in a de facto sense associated with each other. Some may wish to disassociate themselves from actions of their fellow students that they may find morally reprehensible or foolish. Group work stimulates sharing of information so that issues of this sort can be brought to the surface. The Madison course, therefore, required that all projects contain at least two or more students, that the general thrust of each project and specific activities be publicized (for example, on a bulletin board), and that periodic reports from each project be made to the class as a whole.

Teacher Roles

Teachers frequently point to lack of professional preparation for the citizen action curriculum we advocate. This sense of inadequacy is probably due in part to a desire for more substantive knowledge and basic skills in social action itself. The subject, after all, is not part of preparation for teaching. Another facet of the sense of inadequacy may, however, stem from role confusion, for the curriculum model implies a variety of roles for the teacher. In this section, we assume only the practicum context, where major efforts are directed toward student projects, and we identify alternative roles that may present problems for the teacher. These issues are less salient in courses with more conventional classroom or laboratory formats.

General resource. The most common role for a teacher supervising perhaps eight different group projects is to be a general adviser to each group, supplying information on people, places, and resources in the community and on procedures and strategies. As a general facilitator for everyone's project, a resource person cannot become earnestly committed and involved in any one project. Instead, the teacher must be available for anyone who needs help. This might pose a morale problem for a teacher who wishes to take an active part in a specific project, who wishes to develop a special area of expertise rather than a superficial acquaintance with several, or who wants to teach well-defined subject matter or specific skills. In attempting to serve a variety of student projects simultaneously and spontaneously meet each project's educational needs, the role of general resource person makes it almost impossible to fulfill some professional goals.

Even if all of the above personal aspirations were rejected, a teacher might still have difficulty in the role of general resource for social action projects. The role requires considerable knowledge of and personal contacts with a variety of institutions throughout the community. Because teachers spend most of their time with children and other educators, however, they, as an occupational group, remain relatively isolated from contact with the world beyond the school. Physicians, lawyers, salespeople, storekeepers, truck drivers, journalists, and mailmen—all have more opportunity to meet a variety of adults in the course of their daily work than teachers do. For this reason we should not expect teachers to be particularly helpful in putting students in touch with key adults in the community-at-large at the outset. To some extent the problem may be overcome by developing a contingent of more knowledgeable adults willing to help in the role of general resource person.

Counselor. In the role of counselor, as in the role of general resource person, the teacher tries to respond to needs of all students in all projects. But, as counselor, one would be more concerned with emotional or psycho-philosophic dilemmas than with information on community contacts or action strategies. In dealing with emotional aspects of action work (anxiety about perceived risks, ambivalence, frustration with classmates or the system, the disappointment of defeat), the teacher may develop interpersonal relationships with students that can be interpreted more as caring than teaching. There are at least two problems connected with the counselor role. There is a lack of definitive clinical knowledge on how to help students cope with emotional problems salient in social action work. Professional programs in teaching and counseling offer virtually no training in this area. Also, the counseling role faces some of the same difficulties inherent in the general resource role: as a servicer of all students, the teacher cannot become committed to a specific project or teach in a special area of expertise. Teachers who find this important to their professional identity may be dissatisfied with either the counselor or the general resource role.[4]

Expert. Teachers could see themselves as experts in particular substantive areas (environment, racial self-determination, student rights) or type of skill (social research, group organization, public advocacy). Teachers could oversee only those student projects that dealt with their limited areas of expertise. Freed of the superhuman expectation that they must meet everyone's educational needs, teachers can limit efforts to selected topics and find a clearer professional identity, which may be more help to students. Yet there are problems with this role. It requires restricting the range of student projects to topics in areas where the instructor is qualified. This may seem reasonable, but it must also be recognized that, owing to inadequate professional preparation, some teachers may feel totally unqualified as an expert in any area related to citizen action. In the role of expert, moreover, the teacher remains a helper of others rather than an active participant, a distinction that suggests the role of committed activist.

Activist. In this role a teacher declares his or her aim to influence public policy. This might be manifested by joining students already committed to a project or trying to recruit students to one's own group. This pursuit of civic interests is not simply for intellectual clarification, as it is for the expert; it is meant to have public impact. Attention is not divided among diverse sets of issues and students. Rather, the focus is on a single problem, and it is sharpened by working with a single group of students continuously. While the activist role may serve professional and personal needs for continuous, indepth involvement, it gives rise to serious questions. Again we point to deficiencies in teacher preparation. Do we have any reason to believe that teachers are more skilled than students in promoting citizen action efforts? If they are incompetent in an activist role, they could harm rather than help student development in this area. If they became zealously committed to achieving their action goal, they could easily neglect educational responsibilities that must take

---

4. A teacher may, of course, combine the counseling and the general resource roles. We distinguish them here to suggest that they involve different problems in professional preparation.

Choices in Teaching

priority over victory for one's personal cause. The role could trigger vigorous opposition from the community on grounds that the teacher is using students to advance his or her own parochial political interests. To endorse this role and to maintain the political neutrality of the school, it would be necessary for several teachers to participate as activists in conflicting student projects so that it would be clear that a pluralism of political interests was being respected.

Relatively few teachers would choose the activist role, and the profession itself discourages it. The teacher is expected to instruct the young in a relatively private fashion, secluded inside a classroom. The principles of "academic freedom" and "professionalism" deter colleagues and parents from intruding upon the sanctuary. It is the image of teacher as dispassionate inquirer in search of truth (standing above biases and turmoil in public affairs) that constitutes a professional taboo against active involvement. Given the realities of the teaching role, one might even dare to surmise that many teachers choose the profession precisely because they wish to avoid the conflict inherent in advocacy with fellow adults. Apparently many prefer to work in an environment inhabited exclusively by children and fellow educators, an environment in which consensus, support, and love seem more highly valued than conflict or the struggle to exert influence.[5]

Discussions on the Madison course revealed different teacher aspirations as to what ought to be accomplished through student projects. Some were concerned that students learn certain content or skills or something about the complexity of some public issue. Others were less concerned with substantive learning and more interested in students selecting, pursuing, and completing a successful project, regardless of what might be learned through the process. Still others seemed most interested in developing with students a more honest teacher-student relationship, one of mutual trust and respect rather than one based on either the fear or the gamesmanship so frequently observed in conventional teacher-student relations. These aims are not mutually exclusive, but they do seem to account for important differences in teacher opinion about basic goals for a citizen action course. They are summarized as column headings in Table 4.

Even though there are dangers of oversimplification, some of the

---

5. Apple (1971) offers an interesting analysis of conflict versus consensus in curriculum.

TABLE 4
Teacher roles most and least consistent with
major purposes for projects

	Teachers' views of major purpose of project		
Consistency	In-depth study of problem or development of skill	Successful completion of a project	Honest, trusting interpersonal relationships
Most	Expert	Activist	Counselor
	Activist	Resource	Resource
	Resource	Expert	Activist
Least	Counselor	Counselor	Expert

roles discussed above are more or less consistent with each of the teacher concerns. As shown in the table, for example, the expert is most concerned with working on a substantive subject or problem, while the activist mostly wants to get things done and complete a project. In contrast, the counselor, regardless of the student's substantive interests or success in completing a task, wants to focus on the quality of an interpersonal relationship. Space does not permit discussion of all the entries in the table, but, to take another example, the resource person, because of a great concern for the individual projects of all students, is judged to be more consistent with project completion than the expert whose major concern is comprehension or mastery rather than productivity.

This classification leads to no firm conclusions as to which teacher role or concern seems generally preferable to others. Decisions on this matter would depend upon curriculum priorities idiosyncratic to given courses and upon the concerns of individual teachers. The purpose here was to differentiate among alternatives that may not often be apparent so that teachers can identify possible sources of frustration in their roles. We have recognized, but obviously not remedied, many deficiencies in teacher preparation. How such deficiencies might be remedied cannot be intelligently addressed until curriculum development and experimental trials are carried forward in the future.

Evaluating and Grading

Evaluation

Recent attention to educational accountability and renewed controversies over educational testing have generated a literature on educational evaluation far too voluminous to synthesize here. Curriculum evaluation may serve a variety of purposes that might be categorized in different ways, and the collections by Apple *et al.* (1974), Payne (1974), and Walberg (1974) offer useful surveys of the complexity in this field. Evaluation of citizen action curriculum may offer special problems. Before trying to identify those, however, it may help to note that curriculum evaluation in general could conceivably be addressed to any of the following questions:

1. What are the effects of a course (program) on particular constituencies, especially students, teachers, parents, or community agencies?
2. Compared to other courses or educational experiences, has the course in question had a more significant or greater impact on particular constituencies?
3. What particular aspects of the course seemed to result in particular effects (for particular constituencies)?
4. What might be done to improve the course, that is, to maximize beneficial effects and diminish undesirable effects on particular constituencies?

As broad as these questions may seem, they fall short in their implied assumption that evaluation ought to concern itself primarily with assessment of effects of treatments on individual clients or recipients. An alternative perspective would emphasize qualities in the institution or learning environment, regardless of their effects on individual learning (Wehlage *et al.*, 1973). The latter orientation suggests that curriculum developers plan not only for specified effects upon individual people (for example, students, teachers, or parents), but also to create an environment with such characteristics as an informal atmosphere, a democratic structure, rewards for cooperation rather than competition, a tolerance for open inquiry and ambiguity, or a set of clear expectations for student conduct. Though citizen action curriculum should also be evaluated through this orientation, it is necessary, for the moment, to try to clarify alternative approaches to answering the first of the questions regarding the effects of a course upon students.

What areas or types of effects on students is it desirable to assess? A most obvious cluster of effects might be summarized as *proficiency*. Here one wishes to discover what the student has actually learned. Learning can, of course, be subdivided into cognitive knowledge, skills, and attitudes and affect, each perhaps in regard to a variety of topics. Some teachers may be most interested in the mastery of factual knowledge about political process; others, in developing listening skills within a group; others, in building self-confidence. Once a decision is made about which, if any, proficiencies must be mastered by which students, then a procedure for assessing achievement can be devised.[6] Most evaluation schemes emphasize proficiency in "subject matter," usually defined in terms of cognitive knowledge or skills.

A second type of effect, not so well recognized but important in citizen action curriculum, can be called *productivity*. This reflects a concern that projects are successfully completed, that commitments are kept, that "the job gets done." If students choose to publish a special newspaper, then they should actually produce it. If they have chosen to work toward veto of a zoning waiver, then the veto should be closer to reality than when they began. If they decide to form an organization on students' legal rights, then that organization should be functioning. Apart from possible gains in individual proficiency, this criterion holds that a citizen action program should make things happen or help students to produce results.

A third type of effect, independent of proficiency and productivity, is *persistence*. Here value is placed upon hard work, becoming engaged, taking a project seriously, regardless of whether one succeeds in achieving the original goal or in mastering specific competencies. This might be considered an "anti-apathy" dimension, suggesting that a major purpose of citizen action curriculum should be simply to get students responsibly involved in public affairs. According to this criterion, a course would be judged successful for those

---

6. Recall comments under "organization of instruction" which indicate the possibility that proficiency objectives may be set jointly by teacher and student rather than unilaterally by the teacher.

Choices in Teaching

students who, as a result of the curriculum, seemed to try harder or to exert more effort.

Finally, one might be concerned that students feel stimulated, excited, or educationally satisfied, regardless of whether proficiency, productivity or persistence has been demonstrated. Many persons, discouraged with the extent to which schooling has "turned kids off," would settle for a course that provided an enjoyable experience. Those measuring this type of effect would look for various kinds of *pleasure* that students received from a course.

Ideally, we would aim for student progress in each of the four "P's." However, progress on one should not be equated with progress on another. One could conceivably learn proficiencies without completing a successful project, without persisting, and without enjoyment. One could complete a successful project without having gained proficiency, without persisting, and without enjoying it, and so on. Unfortunately, resources are not usually sufficient to pursue all four of these avenues in a course evaluation. Making distinctions among them, however, helps to clarify possible choices when, because of scarce resources, priorities need to be established. We will not argue here which of these facets of evaluation ought to be chosen over others, for this involves lengthy consideration of the ultimate purposes of evaluation and of education itself. The staff in the Madison course found this issue to be extremely difficult, but they did choose, implicitly and without formal justification, to evaluate students primarily in terms of persistence, productivity, and pleasure (in that order), with no systematic effort to evaluate individual student proficiencies.

Having selected one or more of these criteria, one must further specify which kind of information would constitute evidence that the criteria have been met. Data can be gathered by requesting self-report testimony from students on their progress, along with corresponding testimony from others (fellow students, school teachers, parents, community teachers) who observe the students' work. Testimony can also be elicited through interviews and questionnaires that contain both unstructured, open-ended, and highly structured questions. In addition to self-report and testimonial data, one could request that students take specific tests or perform certain tasks that would yield information independent of testimony and self-reports.

Finally, there is a great variety of data generated, not exclusively or ostensibly for the purpose of evaluation, but to proceed with the work of the course: logs and diaries, written and oral reports, minutes of meetings, video and audio recordings of students at work, attendance records, learning contracts. In unobtrusive ways an evaluator can search this material for evidence of student achievement. This demands the creation of an observational scheme and category system to select from the mass of data those items relevant to the four "P's." Each of these procedures raises problems of reliability and validity, and each should be scrutinized with regard to ways in which the evaluation process itself might involve violations of privacy, or might in other ways be harmful to instruction within the course.

In a conventional class where the teacher exerts a high degree of control, it is possible to decide in advance of a lesson which specific learning outcomes will be sought (teaching a definition of prejudice) and to shape the environment accordingly (assign certain readings, discuss certain questions). Because of this degree of control it may be feasible to ask the educator to specify in advance and to assess in a pre-post fashion student progress on specific proficiencies. Participants (student and teachers) in a practicum have less control over learning. Because activities are guided by the many unforeseen events that arise in social action work, it is often impossible to predict in advance specific proficiencies to be gained as a result of a given experience.

For several reasons, then, conventional conceptions of evaluation may be inappropriate for a citizen action curriculum. First, many experiences are selected not because they are believed to contribute to individual proficiencies, but because they may be necessary to complete an important task. (One does not expect to learn much from stuffing envelopes, but one does it for other reasons.) Second, even if one desired that every experience contribute to individual proficiency, in many cases we do not know enough to predict what experiences lead to various proficiencies. (What combination of reading, observation, participation in, and responsibility for running a group meeting, for example, will improve one's leadership skills?) Third, even if we had adequate knowledge as to what kinds of experiences lead to specific proficiencies and the desire to select experiences on that basis, we are often, nevertheless, unable to control the environment sufficiently to ensure that the right kind of variables occur in the right time at the right place. Finally, if all of the above issues could be resolved, an incessant preoccupation with evaluation can defeat the purpose of instruction if students and staff begin to feel that the judgmental function of a course assumes more importance than teaching and learning. In spite of these difficulties, great pressure is often placed upon innovative courses, especially those in which teachers are seen as having less control over students than they would in a conventional class, to demonstrate their effectiveness with regard to student proficiencies. We have tried to show here that concern with student proficiency can be seen as only one aspect of evaluation and that, even if one is highly concerned with this, there are hazards in pursuing evaluation according to the model of prediction and control commonly used in evaluating conventional instruction.[7]

Returning to the broader concept of evaluation outlined in our four original questions, we should recall that there may be constituencies other than students who must benefit before a citizen action program can be judged successful. One justification for community involvement, for example, is provision of services to the community-at-large. If students set out to help groups of people, perhaps the ultimate recipients of student efforts should be evaluated to learn the extent to which they did in fact benefit from student efforts. Using this approach, data would be gathered from the elderly, children, consumers, the poor— whomever an action project was intended to assist. One might also make evaluative inquiries of other constituencies to ascertain, for example, what types of social action projects teachers find most helpful to their own education, what types of involvement parents tend to support, or whether community youth projects seem to have changed adult attitudes toward youth. A comprehensive evaluation scheme could thus consider many questions beyond the obvious attempt to assess the effect of a course on individual students.

Grading

The essential purpose of evaluation, as it has been discussed here, is to assess the effects of instruction. The purpose of grading is to

---

7. Evaluating the effects of conventional instruction is, of course, no simple task. Because of the difficulty of attaining adequate experimental design even in conventional settings, it is often impossible to trace student mastery of specific proficiencies to specific courses or parts thereof.

assign to each student an index representing the extent of his individual achievement with regard to some standardized norm. The grade becomes a matter of public record that can be used to compare the performance of one individual with that of another in terms of a common body of knowledge or a cluster of skills. Clearly, then, one can engage in evaluation without grading students (that is, one could ascertain the effect of an experience on a student without coding that effect into a standardized norm). Conversely, one can grade students without performing evaluation (that is, one could ascertain that a student's level of performance fell in the top 10 percent of a class without knowing whether instruction itself actually caused that performance).

To the extent that grades are not actually based upon standardized norms, they are misleading and meaningless. Suppose Jane and Sue take separate courses in English literature at different high schools. Jane earns a B; Sue, a C. If each course studied different material or if each teacher used different standards to judge student performance, no meaningful comparison could be made between the two. Because of the high likelihood of variation in these matters, therefore, we cannot conclude that Jane knows more than Sue. Nor could we conclude that Jane performed better relative to her classmates than Sue did relative to hers. To reach such a conclusion we would need information on the grades of all other students in each class. It is possible, for example, that Jane's grade was the lowest in her class and Sue's was the highest in her class. About the only conclusion we can draw is that Jane's teacher judged her "good" and Sue's teacher judged her "average" with regard to standards hidden from us. Other powerful critiques of the grading system discuss the way in which it fosters social stratification and denies equal opportunity, inhibits learning, creates a false meritocracy, rewards competition rather than cooperation. Here, the argument is limited to the claim that, because of inevitable variation in instruction and criteria for judging performance, grades do not in practice accomplish their ostensible purpose of providing standardized scaled comparisons in student achievement. They are not derived from standardized norms, or perhaps it is more accurate to say that the norms on which they appear to be based come from populations so small and unique that they are useless as norms.

This problem is most acute in courses where unique learning objectives are established for individual students, and citizen action courses are likely to be of this type. With no standardized norms of knowledge, skills, or attitudes on which to base grades, perhaps they could be based simply on the degree to which individuals succeed in meeting their own idiosyncratic objectives. An A would represent achievement of virtually all objectives that a student set for himself or herself, while a C would represent achievement of, say, only 70 percent of the stated goals. Such an individualized approach to grading is, however, useless in providing any information as to what students actually have learned.

If, for purposes of awarding diplomas or determining when a student has completed a course, it is necessary to keep some public record of student performance, it is reasonable to specify a minimal level of work expected from all students. Work requirements could be hours of class attendance, the writing of documents, preparation of reports, or other activities. Students who meet minimal work requirements would receive credit for the work. Awarding of credit based on minimal types of work or on indications of productivity avoids assessment of proficiency based on invalid norms.

Evidence of student proficiency can be supplied directly through a variety of documents: written essays and reports, photographs, recorded music or conversation, records of programmed instruction completed, testimonial statements from those who have observed student performance, and, if one so desires, even scores on properly standardized tests in the subjects one hopes to master. Direct evidence of student proficiency provides a more accurate assessment of performance than can be supplied through exclusive use of a grading system. The fact that many colleges or employers prefer grades as a quicker method of judging proficiency does no damage to our claim that direct evidence yields a far more accurate assessment.

Thus far we have discussed only the public aspect of grading, or ways of supplying information about student performance to persons other than the student. We must not neglect the importance of evaluation for the individual student. To assist students in making progress toward desired objectives, teachers and colleagues should devote considerable attention to how each is doing, not in terms of comparison with others, but in terms of individual goals. Judgments and discussions of this sort are intended primarily to facilitate learning and, therefore, they have no place in public records. Comments and constructive criticism within the instructional process are critical aspects of evaluation, but they should not be confused with the task of publicly certifying what a student has done or learned.

Our opposition to grading, then, should not be interpreted as opposition to evaluation. Teachers, like other professionals, have an obligation to assess the effects of their actions on "clients." Much of the controversy over grading and evaluation might be resolved if more attention were given to differences among the functions of providing an index of comparison based on truly standardized norms, of certifying completion of minimal amounts of work, of accurately documenting student proficiency, and of giving private evaluative feedback to enhance learning.

With this elaboration of instructional choices added to the many issues in program design, one can reasonably question whether such a curriculum can be successfully introduced into the public secondary school. It may be clearly impossible in some schools. It may involve considerable struggle and development in others. There are schools, however, where it might be incorporated with surprising ease. Because so much remains to be done in the development of curriculum, it would serve no purpose at this point to make a general prediction about the acceptability of this idea on a nation-wide basis. In spite of the problems raised, obstacles do not appear sufficiently great to discourage future development, and the Conclusion suggests specific steps that can be taken.

Conclusion

The Next Step

This book does not offer a fully elaborated curriculum. Rather, it presents a rationale for, and a conception of, curriculum that requires further development prior to attempting large-scale implementation. Development could continue at the local secondary school or district level, or there could be special programs aimed at a broader national constituency. Ideally, it would be helpful to have a national clearinghouse or network to assist local schools in sharing curriculum approaches, materials, program structures, evaluation schemes, to offer training for teachers, and to conduct systematic research on the teaching of citizen action skills. While such a center would be helpful, schools can begin independent efforts immediately.

Interested teachers, administrators, or other educators may launch, as their personal citizen action projects, efforts to persuade local education agencies to support the development of citizen action curriculum. Chapters 1 and 2 have presented an intellectually sound rationale and provided rebuttals to specific points likely to be raised in opposition. According to our model, the educator should then choose particular policy priorities from among a number of alternatives. For example, what course or courses should be developed first? Should teachers request a summer workshop to write materials? Must existing school regulations be changed to allow students more access to the community? When should a citizens' advisory board be established and how should members be selected? Decisions on matters like these will define the way in which the local educator-activist exerts influence in the "public affair" of school curriculum formation.

Because of wide variation in local conditions, we cannot prescribe a priority scheme for what issues ought to be tackled in each project. There are, however, some parts of a development plan that would be most consistent with the thrust of this book.

1. The ultimate objective should be a citizen action curriculum that occupies a significant portion of the student's program (our estimate is four credits or from one-fifth to one-quarter of the major parts of the curriculum). This could be pursued through a long-term plan that would take up to five years and be divided into stages, with one course at a time being developed, tried, and then implemented. Mindful that at present most schools may consider this an excessive focus on citizen action, it may be feasible initially to gain support for only one course. Because of individual differences, some students may need somewhat less time to increase their effectiveness. Within a single course some students may show great progress on a few of the components in the model; other students might thoroughly enjoy a short-term involvement in citizen action and have no desire to increase their effectiveness. On these grounds, the "half-loaf" approach might be justified, but it must be realized that the major goal of increasing effectiveness for most students is not being achieved. It must be clearly understood that the single course is merely a strategic move, not a concession that one course in citizen action is sufficient. Once developed and taught, such a course should be a beginning step in pressing for a more extensive curriculum. Though our position may be disputed, we estimate that most students will significantly increase their ability to exert influence only if at least a four-credit equivalent is provided.

2. In mustering support for citizen action courses, it helps to make connections between this curriculum and educational innovations in other areas. A proposed course on "Taking a Stand: Moral Deliberation and Social Policy Research" can address many recent concerns for values education and moral reasoning. The same course can also help meet familiar demands for critical thinking, inquiry, research skills, and knowledge in social science. As the subject of English becomes increasingly focused on communications skills, a citizen action course on "Winning Support: Persuasion and Group Work" is con-

Conclusion

sistent with that objective. Community involvement activities can also be justified in terms of curriculum goals as diverse as career education or service to the community. In recognizing that citizen action education can converge with other goals in the secondary curriculum, we do not suggest that the other goals take precedence. Unless the development effort remains guided by citizen action competence as the highest priority, it risks becoming diffused, preempted, or generally ineffective in trying to serve too many educational missions.

3. Development projects for specific courses might be directed by a team consisting of a teacher, an experienced, perhaps university-based, curriculum developer, and an adult with extensive citizen action experience. This team should also have continuous contact with advisory consultants such as secondary students and specialists in adolescent psychology and curriculum evaluation. Adequate curriculum development cannot be accomplished by teachers, university developers, or activists in isolation from each other. They must work together and try to incorporate insights from students, curriculum evaluators, and those sensitive to adolescent psychology. All of these parties need not work full time or have an equal and legally binding voice in the development process. The nature of their participation will obviously vary, depending upon the part of the curriculum under consideration. The practicing adult activist, for example, may spend more time on organization-administration-management than on moral deliberation; the psychologist may focus more on psycho-philosophic concerns and group work than on knowledge of the political-legal process.

4. Because teachers have had relatively little experience with citizen action, in-service education should first help them to become involved in their own attempts to exert influence in public affairs, and to reflect upon that experience. This could be accomplished through action workshops for concentrated periods (perhaps six weeks) during the summer or periodic meetings (perhaps twice a month) during the school year. In the workshops teachers would not create a curriculum for children; they would instead immerse themselves in the problems of citizen action as the best way to learn the subject. This field experience would better equip teachers to react to our proposed curriculum. It would serve as a prerequisite for participation in the curriculum development phase or for teaching the citizen action curriculum itself.

This suggestion raises the general question of teacher competence. Earlier remarks (Chapters 2 and 5) noted that teachers seem ill prepared to educate for citizen action. Certainly they cannot rely upon additional university course work to bring them up to date in this field. Concern for teacher ability need not, however, deter curriculum development at this point. There is a reasonably solid knowledge base in the fields of moral deliberation, social policy research, advocacy, and group work. Once this is synthesized into a citizen action education focus, courses on "Taking a Stand" and "Winning Support" could be presented in a relatively structured, self-contained format appropriate for exposition through in-service education. Much learning during the practicum is also comparable to on-the-job training, where students learn by doing and through frequent contact with more experienced adults. In other words, the classroom teacher in this phase would rely heavily on the teaching competence of other adults and youth in the community. The handling of psycho-philosophic concerns is admittedly perhaps the most difficult aspect in this phase, and there is little reason to believe that teachers or others have special competence on these matters. Since one purpose of curriculum development is precisely to identify the kinds of instructional experiences which teachers *can* handle, these difficulties should be seen as proper challenges for development work itself, not as grounds for abandoning the task. With our rationale, general model of curriculum components, bibliography, appendix of illustrative programs and supportive organizations, and with these suggestions, development projects to confront such problems can be initiated by teachers, administrators, parents, and students.

Recapitulation

We have argued that the enhancement of student ability to exert influence in public affairs should be a central objective of the secondary curriculum. After defining and qualifying key terms, we gave two lines of justification. One is the contention that the ability to exert influence in public affairs is a critical aspect of a more general educational goal: environmental competence. We need environmental competence in order to function as moral agents, and we need it to meet psychic needs, the fulfillment of which is requisite to psychological growth. In other words, environmental competence is re-

Conclusion

quired for both ethical and psychological reasons. As one of a conceivably infinite number of environmental competencies, the ability to exert influence in public affairs is further justified through political theory, based on the ideal of consent of the governed. This second part of the rationale supports the consent ideal by using ethical theory on the nature of justice and epistemological theory on procedural requirements for "the search for truth." The goal of increasing ability to exert influence in public affairs is advocated as a task for the entire secondary curriculum, not just social studies. Its primacy in relation to other legitimate educational goals is proposed on the grounds that the school, in contrast to other institutions, may be uniquely qualified to pursue it if certain reforms were to create more school-community interaction.

The conception or model of curriculum aimed toward the objective emphasizes knowledge, skills, and attitudes not commonly taught in schools, even though they are in many cases consistent with existing school objectives. The components of the model shown in Figure 2 (Chapter 2) are derived from an interdisciplinary, competency-based analysis of what is required for individuals to exert influence in public affairs. While the components of moral deliberation, social policy research, political-legal process, and advocacy have some analogues in existing secondary curriculum, relatively new areas for curriculum development at the secondary level are suggested by group dynamics, organization-administration-management, and especially the resolution of psycho-philosophic concerns. Each of these components calls for major efforts in the creation of instructional materials, program structures, and strategies of teaching and counseling.

While this curriculum conception is novel, it could conceivably be introduced into existing secondary schools without radically modifying the existing program. Various components could be organized into a three-course, four-credit sequence that would also meet some existing credit requirements in English, social studies, and other subjects. Our discussion of many program issues (Chapter 4) and choices in teaching (Chapter 5) was intended to show that curriculum development should not be seen merely as a technological problem of creating proper instructional materials for a hypothetical group of students. The development effort must also pay special attention to such problems as selection of students, professional roles for teachers, alternative approaches to evaluation, school-community relations, and the subtle, but powerful, messages communicated by the authority structure and the instructional climate in which the curriculum resides.

The Curriculum Design in Perspective

Though a historical study was not included, this conception of curriculum could represent a novel design in citizenship education. Educators have continuously endorsed the idea of preparing students for active citizen participation, but the design outlined here is unique in at least four ways: It construes citizen participation to mean the ability to exert influence, and it offers a complex definition of this objective. It is more thoroughly justified through ethical, psychological, and political theory than is customary in curriculum proposals. It offers a competency-based conception of what must be taught, based on an interdisciplinary analysis of the process of exerting influence. And, it requires that attention be devoted to the total school milieu, not just the technology of materials development.

This position can be seen as consistent with such other historic educational movements as progressivism, social reconstructionism, or even life adjustment. Admittedly certain commonalities will be found, but commonalities, or consistency with previous movements, do not alone establish equivalence. We may share the progressive commitment to learning based on active student interaction with environment, but our conception of action is subject to rigorous reflection and rejects a totally permissive, child-centered approach. Along with the social reconstructionists, we see the school as having a social-political objective, but our objective is the strengthening of the consent system, rather than specific social goals such as elimination of poverty or improved medical care. We are in accord with the life adjustment school when we emphasize practical knowledge; we part company, however, by insisting that practical knowledge be used to help people affect the world rather than adjust to it. While we leave to others a more careful analysis of relationships between this design and trends in the history of curriculum thought, these distinctions suggest some possible departures from previous rhetoric and scholarship.

Our proposal relates also to such currently visible movements as

Conclusion

competency-based education, and learning environments. The curriculum components were outlined according to a competency-based framework, but with some reluctance, as should have been clear from the earlier discussion on competency-based models (Chapter 3). The major reason for using this framework was analytic: it helps the curriculum developer conceive of the kinds of knowledge, skills, and attitudes which the student may need to exert influence in public affairs. In this sense it provides guidance as to the content or substance of curriculum. Much of the work in competency-based education extends to the listing of numerous behavioral objectives which students are expected to master. Our use of the competency framework stops short of this on the grounds that highly specific behaviors in a curriculum model risk the dangers of trivializing instruction or of excessively manipulating the student. Instead, our notion of competence implies a good deal of student autonomy and responsibility in choosing specific behaviors or competencies to be mastered. In learning advocacy skills, for example, some students may work primarily on oral debate, others on the writing of briefs, and others on the writing of radio spot announcements. One general competency in moral deliberation may be the ability to distinguish between factual and value claims. Students may be instructed in that general type of behavior, but its actual use will be left up to students as they select the particular public policies that require ethical justification. In this sense, we have tried to use a competency model in a manner that avoids endless behavioral objectives handed down by the teacher and preserves student autonomy and responsibility.

Various observers suggest that the real problem of curriculum is the quality of life in schools and that, to reform in any significant way what is being taught, one must first reform the general environment in which teaching and learning occurs. They claim that one cannot teach democracy in an autocratic institution, one cannot teach inquiry to children in an institution where adults do not practice it, and one cannot teach responsibility or cooperation in an institution which denies students the right to make important decisions and encourages them to compete against each other. This concern for effects of the hidden curriculum or the total environment is critical, and curriculum planning should not proceed without taking it into account (see Chapter 4).

At the same time, a useful curriculum design requires more than the establishment of a just institution or a humane environment. We can imagine, for example, a school in which the Bill of Rights is faithfully extended to children; one where children have a significant voice in the governance of the school (including the hiring of teachers); one where the adult instructors possess much up-to-date knowledge, are genuinely interested in the students, and do not feel threatened by them; one where learning is valued intrinsically; one where destructive competition, racism, or any other "undesirable" attitudes are absent. Many would recognize this as an ideal learning environment. Having solved the environmental problem, however, the important question still remains: What should be taught and why? The substance or basic thrust of the curriculum will have to be decided in one way or another, and decisions on these matters are different from, though not independent of, decisions on the nature of the learning environment itself. We have tried to pay careful attention to the significance of the learning environment, but primarily as it relates to the substance of a proposed curriculum. Those who concentrate exclusively on creating a just environment work toward a critically significant goal, but the job is unfinished unless the environment also reinforces a justifiable curriculum design.

To place this curriculum design in social or political perspective, one should recall our major ethical commitment to a notion of justice based on equal respect for every human life. From this commitment comes a belief that a system of consent of the governed offers the most just political mechanism for resolving controversy among conflicting interests. It must be recognized, however, that the consent system in the United States falls far short of the ideal of each citizen having relatively equal ability to exert influence in public affairs. It is possible that weaknesses in the consent system are due to factors (see the Introduction) that cannot be rectified through increased citizen competence. These may have to be attacked through general societal reforms (for example, redistribution of wealth or laws on campaign financing). For reasons offered earlier (Chapter 2), however, the appropriate educational strategy is to help people become more competent in the exercise of influence. In this sense our political goal is participatory democracy, but our position maintains that, for the *educator,* "power" to the people means "competence" to the people to exert influence in public affairs.

Appendix

A. Organizations Supporting Community Involvement Curriculum

The following organizations encourage youth participation in community activities as part of the high school curriculum. They provide program information, newsletters, bibliographies, technical assistance, sponsor conferences, etc. The community involvement they support ranges from learning about specific topics (e.g., law or environment) to developing inquiry skills to volunteer service to social action. Each organization should be contacted for a more complete description of its activity.

A.B.A. Special Committee on Youth Education for Citizenship
American Bar Association
1155 East 60th Street
Chicago, IL 60637
Works to further the expansion of law-related studies at the secondary and elementary school levels.

ACTION
National Student Volunteer Program
806 Connecticut Avenue, NW
Washington, DC 20525
Promotes college and high school volunteer programs through handbooks, teacher and coordinator training sessions, shared information on student volunteer work throughout the United States. Publishes a periodical, the *Synergist*.

Center for a Voluntary Society
1785 Massachusetts Avenue
Washington, DC 20036

Promotes conferences, training, research, and publications relating to the general adult and youth volunteer movement, but no primary focus on the secondary school.

Center for Youth Development and Research
325 Haecker Hall
University of Minnesota
St. Paul, MN 55101

Promotes the use of community resources for learning, particularly through long-term student involvement in public and private community agencies.

Citizenship Education Clearing House
411 N. Elizabeth Avenue
St. Louis, MO 63135

Not a community action program in itself, CECH through a variety of activities sponsors and seeks to further high school programs which involve students directly in the civic life of their communities.

Executive High School Internships of America
680 Fifth Avenue, 9th Floor
New York, NY 10019

Sponsors a semester sabbatical with full academic credit for high school juniors and seniors to become nonpaid special assistants to senior officials of an organization or institution within the local community. Enrolls more than two thousand students from twenty-seven cities in sixteen states.

National Center for Voluntary Action
1625 Massachusetts Avenue, NW
Washington, DC 20036

Promotes volunteerism in general, publishes *Voluntary Action Leadership* and *Voluntary Action News*. No primary focus on the secondary school.

National Commission on Resources for Youth, Inc.
36 West 44th Street
New York, NY 10036

A nonprofit organization begun in 1967, NCRY has two principal functions: the collection and dissemination of information on community involvement programs for youth, and the development of such programs. Among the programs developed on a national scale are "Youth Tutor Youth" and the "Day Care Youth Helper Program." Has published *40 Projects by Groups of Kids, Youth into Adult, New Roles for Youth in the School and Community*. Distributes films and videotapes.

Appendix

B. Directory of Illustrative Youth Community Involvement Projects

The directory lists schools and other organizations that operate community involvement projects for youth as of 1974. This is not an exhaustive list of all such projects in the United States but an illustrative sample compiled from information received from many of the organizations listed in Part I.* Because of the rapid emergence of new projects and the termination of old ones, such a directory quickly becomes dated. Nevertheless, it portrays a general sense of the nature of community involvement related to secondary education and specific addresses toward which to direct further inquiry.

The projects vary in their purposes according to headings given below. The categorization is based in many cases on brief and possibly incomplete information, and many projects fall into more than one category. In spite of these problems, rough distinctions such as the following have been made with regard to their primary goals:

I. Volunteer service (school sponsored)
  Ia. Volunteer service emphasizing tutoring
II. Volunteer service (sponsored by other agencies)
III. Field research
IV. Career exploration (school sponsored)
  IVa. Career exploration (sponsored by other agencies)
V. Social action
VI. Course enrichment
VII. Youth services
VIII. Multidistrict or statewide programs

A brief introduction to each category offers general information about programs in its class. Additional annotation is given to indicate exceptions to the general pattern or to supply other information. Entries are arranged within each category, alphabetically by school and state.

I. Volunteer Service (school sponsored)

Many of the school-sponsored projects place student volunteers in such local agencies as hospitals, nursing homes, day-care centers, or other schools. Students generally receive academic credit for volunteer service as part of either required or elective course work. In some instances such service is required for graduation. Volunteer service projects are often connected with classroom instruction. A book, *High School Courses with Volunteer Components* (ACTION, National Student Volunteer Program, Part I), describes twelve additional programs, but does not supply specific school names and addresses.

*Examples of publications consulted were: *40 Projects by Groups of Kids* and *Youth into Adult* (National Commission on Resources for Youth), the *Synergist* (ACTION, National Student Volunteer Program), *Twenty-Five Action Learning Schools* (National Association of Secondary School Principals).

Appendix

1. Beverly Hills High School
   Beverly Hills, CA 90212

2. Evanston Township High School
   Community Service Seminar
   Evanston, IL 60201

3. Lake Forest Academy—Ferry Hall
   Lake Forest, IL 60056

4. Niles North High School
   9800 Lawler Avenue
   Skokie, IL 60076
   Students do volunteer work as part of an independent study course in the social studies.

5. West High School
   Iowa City, IA 52240
   Rather than take part in regular physical education classes, students may volunteer to aid specialists conducting exercise sessions at a local retirement home.

6. Topeka High School
   Topeka, KS 66612

7. Mercy High School
   Baltimore, MD 21210

8. Andover High School
   Andover, MA 01810

9. East Lansing High School
   East Lansing, MI 48823

10. Hoffman High School
    Hoffman, MN 56339

11. Eisenhower High School, Lindbergh High School
    Hopkins, MN 55343

12. North High School
    Minneapolis, MN 55440

13. Northrop Collegiate School
    Minneapolis, MN 55440

14. Regina High School
    Minneapolis, MN 55440

15. Montville Township High School
    100 Horseneck Road
    Montville, NJ 07045

16. John Dewey High School
    50 Avenue X
    Brooklyn, NY 11223

Appendix 173

17. McQuaid Jesuit High School
    1800 Clinton Avenue, South
    Rochester, NY 14618

18. Spring Valley High School
    Spring Valley, NY 10977

19. Herbert W. Schroeder High School
    Webster, NY 14580

20. Wissabicken High School
    Ambler, PA 19002

21. Waynesboro High School
    Waynesboro, PA 17268

22. Belle Fourche High School
    Belle Fourche, SD 57717
    Students, participating in a "Youth Conservation Corps" set up by the U.S. Department of the Interior, work on conservation projects.

23. Oak Ridge High School
    Oak Ridge, TN 37830

24. Bishop Dunne High School
    3900 Rugged Drive
    Dallas, TX 75224
    Students do not receive academic credit for volunteer service; rather, each student must participate in such a project in order to graduate.

25. Mariner High School
    Everett, WA 98204
    All students in the school are required to participate in volunteer service at community agencies.

26. Hudson Bay High School
    Vancouver, WA 98660

27. Memorial High School
    Gammon Road
    Madison, WI 53705

28. Winnequah Middle School
    Monona, WI 53716
    Middle school students work with a number of community agencies without receiving academic credit.

29. West Bend East and West High Schools
    West Bend, WI 53095

Ia. Volunteer Service Emphasizing Tutoring

A number of volunteer service projects place major emphasis on adolescents tutoring younger children. The high school students usually receive academic credit for their work in the subjects they teach which vary from mathematics to improvisational drama.

1. Berkeley High School
   2246 Milvia Street
   Berkeley, CA 94704

2. George Washington High School
   Richmond District
   San Francisco, CA 94101

3. Cherry Creek School District
   4700 South Yosemite
   Englewood, CO 80110

4. Calvin Coolidge High School
   Washington, DC 20005

5. Ridgewood High School
   Norridge, IL 60690

6. Red Wing State Training School
   Red Wing, MN 55066
   Through a project entitled "Institution Community Continuum Program," young delinquents plan and direct activities for a group of mentally and physically handicapped children.

7. Central High School
   St. Paul, MN 55175
   In two separate programs, students in regular biology classes teach elementary school children, and other students teach music and drama to the same age group.

8. Stillwater Public Schools
   Stillwater, MN 55082
   Through a social studies course entitled "School and Community," high school students work as tutors in elementary schools.

9. St. John's High School
   Toledo, OH 45501
   As part of a social studies course in child development and education, high school students tutor children at an inner-city grade school.

II. Volunteer Service (sponsored by other agencies)

Many adolescents work in volunteer projects not directly related to the school curriculum, but in some cases the school may serve as a common meeting ground for coordination and discussion.

1. Students Work with the Handicapped
   c/o Cameron School
   El Cerrito, CA 94530
   Junior high students, in off-school hours, provide company and recreation for handicapped elementary school children.

Appendix

2. Institute for Educational Development
   999 North Sepulveda Boulevard
   El Segundo, CA 90245
   Teenagers, after preservice training, teach small children at a day-care center.

3. McClymond's Youth Council
   2516 Filbert Street
   Oakland, CA 94607
   Members of the Youth Council operate a camp in rural California for inner-city children aged eight to twelve.

4. Youth for Service
   804 Mission Street
   San Francisco, CA 94103
   Former delinquents in San Francisco's Chinatown provide material aid for poor inner-city residents.

5. Adopt a Grandparent
   State of Connecticut, Department on Aging
   90 Washington Street
   Hartford, CT 06115
   Students perform various volunteer services for the elderly.

6. Black Liberation School
   Thomas Moorehead, Director
   Project Community
   Student Services Bldg. 2210
   University of Michigan
   Ann Arbor, MI 48401
   High School students are among the volunteers at the Black Liberation School, an educational enrichment project for children attending elementary and junior high schools in Michigan's Washtenaw County.

7. Children's Art Bazaar Art Gallery
   5229 Columbia Avenue
   St. Louis, MO 63139
   Students, in conjunction with professionals from the community, manage a gallery which exhibits artwork by children from the community.

8. Students Concerned with Public Health
   615 Spruce Street
   Philadelphia, PA 19106
   Young people make presentations on public health to elementary school children.

III. Field Research

Through field research outside the school, teachers seek to increase students' knowledge about community affairs and to improve their skills in gathering and interpreting information. In some cases the students' findings are communicated to local officials as evidence for the need for governmental action in a particular area.

1. Enfield High School
   Social Studies Laboratory
   Enfield, CT 06082
   Students operate a Social Studies Laboratory, which serves as a center for extracurricular research into a wide variety of social topics.

2. Ames High School
   20th and Ridgewood
   Ames, IA 50010
   In social studies courses, art classes, and independent study courses, students do field research in the community.

3. Bedford High School
   Bedford, MA 01730
   As part of the Problems of Democracy Course for twelfth graders, students spend four weeks researching some aspect of conflict in contemporary society.

4. Oliver Ames High School
   North Easton, MA 02356
   Through a senior year elective course entitled "Local History," students research their community's past against the background of United States history.

5. The Equal Justice Council
   462 Gratiot Street
   Detroit, MI 48226
   Through the "Court Watchers" program, a nonschool activity, teenagers attend court sessions in Detroit and compile data on the handling of criminal cases.

6. Oakland Schools
   2100 Pontiac Lake Road
   Pontiac, MI 48054
   Students in grades nine through twelve learn field research methodology and conduct research programs dealing with social issues in their own communities.

7. Central Junior High School
   Alexandria, MN 56308
   In a ninth-grade course, "American Political Behavior," students conduct field research in their community and through their findings participate in community affairs.

8. New City School
   St. Paul, MN 55175
   Students, following training in lab techniques and research procedures, take a trip on the Mississippi River, investigating and documenting the history and ecology of the river. In another course students seek out various aspects of local history and publish their accounts in a magazine entitled *Scattered Seeds*.

Appendix

9. University City School District
   725 Kingsland Avenue
   University City, MO 63130
   As part of a unit of study entitled "Studies in the Environment: Redesigning the Community," junior high school students do field research in their community.

10. Pascack Hills High School
    Montvale, NJ 07045
    In a U.S. history course required for all eleventh and twelfth graders, students may elect to do research in the community on a variety of contemporary problems.

11. Whitmer High School
    5601 Clegg Drive
    Toledo, OH 43613
    Students conduct field research in the community as part of a "Survival Curriculum" program offered to eleventh and twelfth graders.

12. Philadelphia Historical Commission
    Room 1313
    City Hall Annex
    Philadelphia, PA 19107
    Teenagers, in an activity not related to schoolwork, research aspects of black history in the city of Philadelphia.

13. Parker Senior High School
    3125 Mineral Point Avenue
    Janesville, WI 53545
    As part of the school's integrated social studies curriculum, students work on field research projects.

IV. Career Exploration (school sponsored)

Community involvement can stimulate vocational or career exploration by facilitating on-the-job apprenticeships and internships with experienced adults. Many of these carry academic credit.

1. Pacific High School
   Apprenticeship Training Program
   Box 908
   Montara, CA 94037

2. Manual High School
   Denver, CO 80201
   Industrial arts students learn skills through community projects, such as housing construction, sidewalk repair, and work in hospitals and schools.

3. Cooperative Education Program
   New York University Medical Center
   and
   Joan of Arc Junior High School
   550 First Avenue
   New York, NY 10016
   Through work at the New York University Medical Center, ninth-grade science students explore careers in medicine.

4. Champlain Valley Union High School
   Hinesburg, VT 05461

5. Nicolet High School
   6701 North Port Washington Road
   Milwaukee, WI 53217

IVa. Career Exploration (sponsored by other agencies)

Frequently nonschool agencies establish their own career exploration programs for youth.

1. High School Mental Health Careers Program
   c/o Massachusetts Association for Mental Health
   38 Chauncey Street
   Boston, MA 02111
   Volunteers work at mental hospitals.

2. Architectural Skills Training Program
   Washington University
   St. Louis, MO 63130
   Under the direction of architecture students at Washington University, young people work on building projects for the community.

3. Seattle Neighborhood Youth Corps
   Dental Project
   Seattle, WA 98101
   Neighborhood Youth Corps enrollees assist dentists.

V. Social Action

Social or citizen action programs involve students in direct attempts to influence the policy or the quality of service of public institutions. As a first step in action projects, students often choose to inform the community about the existence of a problem and the need for action.

1. Campolindo High School
   Moraga, CA 94556
   In "Project Earth," students organize to improve community awareness about environmental problems.

2. New City School
   400 Sibley Street
   St. Paul, MN 55101

Appendix

Students participate in political action groups, work with legal aid and public assistance programs, and survey the natural and urban environments with emphasis on research and social action.

3. St. Paul Open School
   St. Paul, MN 55175
   Students in an ecology class seek out the sources of pollution, and, through a variety of means, campaign for enforcement of antipollution laws.

4. New Jersey Student Union
   97 Church Street
   New Brunswick, NJ 08901
   Seventh- through twelfth-grade students conduct programs concentrating on student rights, including lectures, debates, student participation in decision making, and extracurricular activities.

5. Institute for Political-Legal Education
   P.O. Box 426
   Glassboro Woodbury Road
   Pitman, NJ 08071
   Operating in some fifteen high schools in New Jersey, the Institute's program is designed to acquaint students with the opportunities for participation in the political process. Offered as a social studies elective for eleventh and twelfth graders, the program provides internships at the state and federal government levels and a variety of activities involving students in political affairs.

6. The Hudson Guild Study Den
   441 West 26th Street
   New York, NY 10016
   Teenagers, trained to identify housing code violations, survey neighborhood dwellings to inform tenants of their rights to seek correction of violations.

7. New York City Health Information Project
   255 East Houston Street
   New York, NY 10002
   Teenage volunteers help to educate the community about health problems, with particular emphasis on the causes, symptoms, and treatment of venereal disease.

8. Northport High School
   Northport, NY 11768
   In social studies classes, students participate in the activities of Amnesty International, an organization formed to free political prisoners throughout the world.

VI. Course Enrichment

While all community involvement projects aim to offer a more enriched learning experience, programs in the above categories indicate a clear focus on either volunteer service, research, or social action. Many involvement programs are less easily categorized, for they may combine a number of approaches, yet share the common goal of sharpening students' social awareness.

1. Colton High School
   Colton, CA 92324
   A variety of opportunities for off-campus involvement are offered, including tutoring programs, credit for courses in English, government, and consumer economics, and opportunities for career exploration.

2. Salinas Union High School District-Alisal High School
   Salinas, CA 93901
   The Community Laboratory in Political Science, a combination of classroom work in government and exploratory work experience with government agencies, seeks to provide students with a better understanding of the actual operations of government.

3. Lowell High School
   1101 Eucalyptus Drive
   San Francisco, CA 94132
   Through the "Basic Law Workshop," an elective course which partly fulfills the civics requirement for graduation, twelfth-grade students participate in a number of law-related activities, including field trips to courts and prisons, ride-along programs with the local police, and a community internship program.

4. Moreno Valley High School
   Sunnymead, CA 92388
   In an elective semester course entitled "Law for Everyday Living," students take field trips to courts and prisons, and participate in other activities designed to increase knowledge about the legal process.

5. Rabun Gap High School
   Rabun Gap, GA 30568
   Students in grades eight through twelve, as part of an elective journalism class, publish the national quarterly magazine, *Foxfire*. Among other topics, *Foxfire* publishes articles about the people of this Appalachian Mountain region.

6. Mundelein High School
   1350 West Hawley Street
   Mundelein, IL 60060
   To develop a better understanding of government, all students are required to participate in a public activity, such as volunteer work for community agencies, attendance at public meetings, or service on community youth councils.

7. Maine Reach
   Chewonki Foundation
   Wiscasset, ME 04578
   In a privately funded program, eleventh and twelfth graders and high school graduates live together for nine months, going on wilderness trips, working as interns, and taking part in major group action projects. Approved by the state of Maine, Maine Reach provides academic credit when the student's regular school judges that the program is an appropriate alternative.

Appendix

8. Springfield School Department
   195 State Street
   Springfield, MA 01103
   As part of a sixth-grade social studies course, students study the city of Springfield through the use of field trips and special assembly programs.

9. Worcester Academy—Department of Urban Affairs
   Worcester, MA 01604
   As part of a course entitled "Urban Affairs," students work as interns in community agencies and businesses.

10. Lindbergh High School
    Hopkins, MN 55343
    An elective course for seniors, "Humanities Outreach" offers volunteer experience, field trips, and seminar discussions in order to expand students' community awareness.

11. Central High School
    Minneapolis, MN 55440
    In a full-year social studies course entitled "The Dynamics of Aging in America," students study the role of the elderly in society, spending their class time three days a week at a neighborhood center for the elderly. Two days a week they discuss the aging process in class.

12. West High School
    Minneapolis, MN 55440
    Social studies students receive field placements with organizations seeking to improve the urban environment.

13. Armstrong High School
    Robbinsdale, MN 55422
    As part of their twelfth-grade social studies course work, students work at community agencies.

14. New City School
    St. Paul, MN 55175
    Through a high school social studies class, "Public Service Video," students operate a public access video network offering videotape production and distribution to the public.

15. Tower Heights Middle School
    Centerville, OH 45459
    In the Independent Learning Program, middle-school students elect to substitute outside projects for regular classroom work in one, two, or all curricular areas.

16. The Fourth Street "i"
    c/o Brigade in Action
    136 Avenue C
    New York, NY 10009
    Teenagers publish a community magazine, *The Fourth Street "i,"* which discusses neighborhood problems. Many copies are mailed to subscribers all

over the country; others are used as supplementary reading in the neighborhood's schools.

VII. Youth Services

Youth have initiated, outside the schools, a number of service projects to help "youth in trouble," facing problems of drugs, delinquency, family conflict, running away, etc. Below are a few of the many youth-led efforts to offer counseling and other resources to their peers.

1. Crisis Intervention
Rio Hondo Crises Intervention Council
P. O. Box 593
Pico Rivera, CA 90660
Volunteers handle a telephone center, providing support for young people who need emergency aid and advice.

2. "Number Nine"
266 State Street
New Haven, CT 06510
A crisis center initiated and managed by young people, Number Nine is designed to provide services for troubled youth.

3. Encounter, Incorporated
150 Spring Street
New York, NY 10012
A voluntary drug treatment program, Encounter, Incorporated, was developed by teenagers in Greenwich Village.

VIII. Multidistrict or Statewide Programs

Some community involvement programs reach beyond one school, or one school district, and are coordinated by regional agencies at local or state level. Such programs may include several of the types of community involvement already listed.

1. Chicago Board of Education—Project Wingspread
Chicago, IL 60601
Project Wingspread attempts to increase understanding between students in Chicago city schools and those in the city's suburbs. Students participate in learning exchanges between schools.

2. Institute for Political-Legal Education
P. O. Box 426
Glassboro Woodbury Road
Pitman, NJ 08071
Operating in some fifteen high schools in New Jersey, the Institute's program is designed to acquaint students with opportunities for participation in the political process. Offered as a social studies elective for eleventh and twelfth graders, the program provides about four hundred internships at the state and federal government levels and a variety of activities involving students in political affairs.

Appendix 183

3. GRASP
   681 Center Street, N.E.
   Salem, OR 93701
   In the GRASP (Governmental Responsibility and Student Participation) program, twelfth-grade students in Marion County, Oregon, intern in government agencies at the city, county, and state levels, working on research projects, lobbying, drafting legislation, and reporting to other school classes.

4. DUO
   State Department of Education
   Office of the Commissioner
   Montpelier, VT 05602
   DUO ("Do Unto Others") allows tenth- and eleventh-grade students to earn academic credit through a semester-long service project of their choice. Any secondary school in the state may participate.

C. Citizen Action Organizations

Numerous organizations involved in direct citizen action may be helpful to the educator in developing curricula. Through newsletters and other publications, these groups provide (a) information on issues and actions not often covered in the general media; (b) case studies of successful action projects; (c) lists of key resources (people, publications, organizations, funds) on specific issues; (d) suggested strategies for action on particular problems; (e) legal assistance. The list below in no way exhausts all the citizen action groups that might conceivably be helpful, but information from this limited set will provide the foundation for a library of citizen action materials, many of which might be incorporated into a school curriculum. The groups will vary considerably in the kind of resources they offer.

The American Civil Liberties
  Union Foundation
156 Fifth Avenue
New York, NY 10010

Appalachian Research and
  Defense Fund
1116-B Kanawha Blvd. E.
Charleston, WV 25301

Center for Constitutional Rights
588 Ninth Avenue
New York, NY 10036

Center for Educational Reform
2119 S Street, NW
Washington, DC 20008

The Center for Law in the
  Public Interest
P. O. Box 24367
Los Angeles, CA 90024

The Center for Law and Social
  Policy
1751 N Street, NW
Washington, DC 20036

Center for Public Representation
520 University Avenue
Madison, WI 53703

Center for Science in the
  Public Interest
1779 Church St., NW
Washington, DC 20036

Appendix

Center for the Study of
 Responsive Law
P. O. Box 19367
Washington, DC

Citizen Action Group
2000 P Street, NW
Washington, DC 20036

Citizens Advocate Center
211 Connecticut Avenue
Washington, DC

Citizens Communication Center
1816 Jefferson Place, NW
Washington, DC

Common Cause
2030 M Street, NW
Washington, DC 20036

Corporate Information Center
475 Riverside Drive
New York, NY 10027

Council on Economic Priorities
456 Greenwich St.
New York, NY 10013

Environmental Action
1346 Connecticut Avenue
Washington, DC 20036

Environmental Defense Fund
162 Old Town Road
East Setauket, LI, NY 11733

Environmental Law Institute
Dupont Circle Bldg.-Suite 614
1346 Connecticut Avenue, NW
Washington, DC 20036

Institute for Public Interest
 Representation
Georgetown Law Center
506 E Street
Washington, DC 20001

Institute for Responsive
 Education
704 Commonwealth Avenue
Boston, MA 02215

Law Students Civil Rights
 Research Council
156 Fifth Avenue
New York, NY 10010

Lawyers Committee for Civil
 Rights Under Law
733 15th Street, NW
Washington, DC

League of Women Voters
 Education Fund
1730 M Street, NW
Washington, DC

Legal Action Center
271 Madison Avenue
New York, NY 10016

Louisiana Center for the Public Interest
1114 1/2 Royal Street
New Orleans, LA 70116

Mexican American Legal Defense and
 Education Fund
145 Ninth Street
San Francisco, CA 94103

Migrant Services Foundation
395 N.W. First Street
Miami, FL 33128

N.A.A.C.P. Legal Defense and
 Educational Fund
10 Columbus Circle
New York, NY 10019

National Committee for Citizens
 in Education
Suite 410, Wilde Lake Village Green
Columbia, MD 21044

National Prison Law Project
1424 16th Street, NW-Suite 404
Washington, DC 20036

National Wildlife Federation
1412 16th Street, NW
Washington, DC 20036

National Urban League
55 E. 52nd Street
New York, NY

Appendix

Native American Rights Fund
1506 Broadway
Boulder, CO 80302

Natural Resources Defense
  Council, Inc.
1710 N Street, NW
Washington, DC 20036
and
15 W. 44th Street
New York, NY 10036

Pacific Legal Foundation
445 Capitol Mall
Sacramento, CA 95814

Project on Corporate Responsibility
1525 18th Street, NW
Washington, DC 20036

Public Citizen
1346 Connecticut Ave., NW
Washington, DC 20036

Public Law Education Institute
Dupont Circle Bldg.-Suite 610
1346 Connecticut Ave., NW
Washington, DC 20036

Retired Professional Action Group
2000 P Street, NW
Washington, DC 20036

Scientists' Institute for
  Public Information
30 East 68th Street
New York, NY 10021

Sierra Club
1050 Mills Tower
San Francisco, CA 94104

Southern Conference Educational
  Fund
3210 W. Broadway
Louisville, KY 40211

Stern Community Law Firm
2005 L Street
Washington, DC

Tax Analysts and Advocates
732 17th Street, NW
Washington, DC 20006

Urban Planning Aid, Inc.
639 Massachusetts Ave.
Cambridge, MA 02139

Washington Research Project
1763 R Street, NW
Washington, DC

References

Adelson, Joseph, and Robert O'Neill. "The Development of Political Thought in Adolescence: The Sense of Community." *Journal of Personality and Social Psychology*, 43, 1966, 295-306.
Alinsky, Saul. *Rules for Radicals: A Practical Primer for Realistic Radicals.* New York: Random House, 1971.
Allen, Herb, Elliott Buchdruker, David Fuller, JoAnn Silverstein, Ida Strickland, and Tom Silk. *The Bread Game.* San Francisco: Glide Publications, 1973.
Almond, Gabriel A., and Sidney Verba. *The Civic Culture: Political Attitudes and Democracy in Five Nations.* Boston: Little, Brown, 1963.
Apple, Michael W. "The Hidden Curriculum and the Nature of Conflict." *Interchange*, 2:4, 1971, 27-40.
Apple, Michael W., Michael J. Subkoviak, and Henry S. Lufler, Jr. (eds.). *Educational Evaluation: Analysis and Responsibility.* Berkeley: McCutchan, 1974.
Ariés, Philippe. *Centuries of Childhood.* New York: Random House, 1962.
Baier, Kurt. *The Moral Point of View.* New York: Random House, 1965.
Berelson, Bernard, Paul F. Lazarsfeld, and William N. McPhee. *Voting: A Study of Opinion Formulation in a Presidential Campaign.* Chicago: University of Chicago Press, 1954.
Beyer, Barry K. *Inquiry in the Social Studies Classroom.* Columbus, Ohio: Charles E. Merrill, 1971.
Brand, Myles (ed.). *The Nature of Human Action.* Glenview, Ill.: Scott, Foresman, 1970.
Campbell, Angus, Gerald Gurin, and Warren E. Miller. *The Voter Decides.* Evanston, Ill.: Row, Peterson, 1954.
Center for New Schools. "Strengthening Alternative High Schools." *Harvard Educational Review*, 42:3, August 1972, 313-350.
Chapin, June R., and Richard E. Gross. *Teaching Social Studies Skills.* Boston: Little, Brown, 1973.

Chesler, Mark, Bryant Bunyan, James Crowfoot, and Simon Wittes. *Resources for School Change. I: A Manual on Issues and Programs in Training Educational Change.* U.S. Department of Health, Education and Welfare, Office of Education, Bureau of Research and Educational Change Team, School of Education, University of Michigan, Ann Arbor, 1972.

Citizenship Education Project. *Laboratory Practices in Citizenship Education for College Students.* New York: Teachers College, Columbia University, 1955.

Coleman, James S. "How Do the Young Become Adults." *Review of Educational Research,* 42:4, Fall 1972(a), 431-439.

———. *Policy Research in the Social Sciences.* Morristown, N.J.: General Learning, 1972(b).

———, Ernest Q. Campbell, Carol J. Hobson, James McPartland, Alexander M. Mood, Frederic D. Weinfeld, and Robert L. York. *Equality of Educational Opportunity.* Washington: Superintendent of Documents, Government Printing Office, 1966.

Community Press Features. *Open the Books: How to Research a Corporation.* Cambridge, Mass.: Urban Planning Aid, 1974.

Community Research and Publications Group. *People before Property: A Real Estate Primer and Research Guide.* Cambridge, Mass.: Urban Planning Aid, 1972.

Conrad, Dan. *Putting It Together: Learning and Developing through Volunteer Service.* Minneapolis: Center for Youth Development and Research, University of Minnesota, 1973.

Cox, Fred M., John L. Erlich, Jack Rothman, and John E. Tropman (eds.). *Strategies of Community Organization: A Book of Readings.* Itasca, Ill.: F. E. Peacock, 1974.

Crabtree, Charlotte. "Supporting Reflective Thinking in the Classroom," in Jean Fair and Fannie R. Shaftel (eds.), *Effective Thinking in the Social Studies.* 37th Yearbook, National Council for the Social Studies, Washington, D.C., 1967, pp. 77-122.

Dewey, John (1916). *Democracy and Education.* New York: Free Press, 1966.

——— (1938). *Experience and Education.* New York: Collier, 1973.

Dowtin, Kenneth. "To Build Collective Commitment: A Model for Curriculum Development in Secondary Social Studies." Unpublished dissertation, University of Wisconsin, Madison, 1973.

Erikson, Erik H. "Identity and the Life Cycle." *Psychological Issues,* 1:1, 1959.

———. *Childhood and Society.* New York: Norton, 1960.

———. *Identity: Youth and Crisis.* New York: Norton, 1968.

Fraenkel, Jack R. *Helping Students Think and Value: Strategies for Teaching the Social Studies.* Englewood Cliffs, N.J.: Prentice-Hall, 1973.

Frankena, William K. *Ethics.* Englewood Cliffs, N.J.: Prentice-Hall, 1963.

Freire, Paulo. *Pedagogy of the Oppressed.* New York: Herder and Herder, 1970.

Fried, Edrita. *Active/Passive: The Crucial Psychological Dimension.* New York: Harper and Row, 1970.

Gardner, John W. *In Common Cause: Citizen Action and How It Works.* New York: Norton, 1972.

References

Gillespie, Judith A., and John J. Patrick. *Comparing Political Experiences*. Washington, D.C.: American Political Science Association, 1974.

Gottlieb, David. "The Socialization and Politicization of Vista Volunteers: Sex and Generational Differences." *Journal of Voluntary Action Research*, 3:1, 1974, 1-9.

Greene, Jon S. (ed.). *Grantsmanship: Money and How to Get It*. Orange, N.J.: Academic Media, 1973.

Hampden-Turner, Charles. *Radical Man: The Process of Psycho-Social Development*. Cambridge, Eng.: Schenkman, 1970.

Hampshire, Stuart. *Thought and Action*. New York: Viking, 1959.

Hare, Richard M. *Freedom and Reason*. London: Oxford University Press, 1963.

Holden, Matthew. "Politics and Voluntary Social Action: Some Rules of Thumb." *Journal of Voluntary Action Research*, 2:1, January 1973, 48-59.

Huenefeld, John. *The Community Activist's Handbook: A Guide for Citizen Leaders and Planners*. Boston: Beacon, 1970.

Hunt, Maurice P., and Lawrence E. Metcalf. *Teaching High School Social Studies*. New York: Harper and Row, 1968.

Jencks, Christopher, Marshall Smith, Henry Acland, Mary Jo Bane, David Cohen, Herbert Gentis, Barbara Heyns, and Stephen Michelson. *Inequality: A Reassessment of the Effect of Family and Schooling in America*. New York: Basic Books, 1972.

Jones, W. Ron. *Finding Community: A Guide to Community Research and Action*. Palo Alto, Calif.: James E. Freel and Assoc., 1971.

Kahn, Si. *How People Get Power: Organizing Oppressed Communities for Action*. New York: McGraw-Hill, 1970.

Kanter, Rosabeth M. *Commitment and Community: Communes and Utopias in Sociological Perspective*. Cambridge, Mass.: Harvard University Press, 1972.

Kaplan, Abraham. *The Conduct of Inquiry: Methodology for Behavioral Science*. San Francisco: Chandler, 1964.

Kohlberg, Lawrence. "Stage and Sequence: The Cognitive-Developmental Approach to Socialization," in David A. Goslin (ed.), *Handbook of Socialization Theory and Research*. Chicago: Rand McNally, 1969, pp. 347-480.

_____. "From Is to Ought: How to Commit the Naturalistic Fallacy and Get Away With It in the Study of Moral Development," in T. Mischel (ed.) *Cognitive and Developmental Epistemology*. New York: Academic Press, 1971.

_____, and Rochelle Mayer. "Development as the Aim of Education." *Harvard Educational Review*, 42:4, November 1972, 449-496.

Lamm, Zvi. "The Status of Knowledge in the Radical Concept of Education," in David E. Purpel and Maurice Belanger (eds.), *Curriculum and the Cultural Revolution*. Berkeley: McCutchan, 1972.

Leming, James S. "Adolescent Moral Judgment and Deliberation on Classical and Practical Moral Dilemmas." Unpublished dissertation, University of Wisconsin, Madison, 1973.

———. "Moral Reasoning, Sense of Control and Social-Political Activism among Adolescents." *Adolescence,* 1974, in press.

Lockwood, Alan. "Stage of Moral Reasoning in Students' Analysis of Public Value Controversy." Unpublished dissertation, Harvard Graduate School of Education, Cambridge, Mass., 1970.

———. "A Critical View of Values Clarification." *Teachers College Record,* in press.

Luft, Joseph. *Group Processes: An Introduction to Group Dynamics.* Palo Alto: National Press, 1970.

Lurie, Ellen. *How to Change the Schools: A Parents' Action Handbook on How to Fight the System.* New York: Vintage, 1970.

McKay, Bridge. *Training for Nonviolent Action for High School Students: A Handbook.* Philadelphia: Friends Peace Committee, 1971.

Marian, Bert, David Rosen, and David Osborne. *How to Research the Power Structure of Your Secondary School System.* Lincoln, Neb.: Study Commission on Undergraduate Education and the Education of Teachers, 1973.

Marsh, David. "Education for Political Involvement: A Pilot Study of 12th Graders." Unpublished dissertation, University of Wisconsin, Madison, 1973.

Maslow, Abraham H. *Motivation and Personality.* New York: Harper and Row, 1954.

Massachusetts Advocacy Center and Massachusetts Law Reform Institute. *Making Schools Work: An Education Handbook for Students, Parents, and Professionals.* Boston: Massachusetts Advocacy Center, 2 Park St., 1974.

Massialas, Byron, and C. Benjamin Cox. *Inquiry in Social Studies.* New York: McGraw-Hill, 1966.

Matthews, Donald R., and James W. Prothro. *Negroes and the New Southern Politics.* New York: Harcourt, Brace, 1966.

Merelman, Richard M. "The Development of Policy Thinking in Adolescence." *American Political Science Review,* 65:4, December 1971, 1033-1047.

Michael, James R. (ed.). *Working on the System: A Comprehensive Manual for Citizen Access to Federal Agencies.* New York: Basic Books, 1974.

Milbrath, Lester W. *Political Participation.* Chicago: Rand McNally, 1965.

Miles, Matthew. *Learning to Work in Groups.* New York: Teachers College, Columbia University Press, 1959.

Mosteller, Frederick, and Daniel Moynihan. *On Equality of Educational Opportunity.* New York: Random House, 1972.

Myrdal, Gunnar. "Mass Passivity in America." *Center Magazine,* 7:2, 1974, 72-75.

Nader, Ralph, and Donald Ross. *Action for a Change: A Student's Manual for Public Interest Organizing.* New York: Grossman, 1971.

National Commission on Resources for Youth. *New Roles for Youth in the School and the Community.* New York: Citation Press, 1974.

Newmann, Fred M. "Consent of the Governed and Citizenship Education in Modern America." *School Review,* 71:4, 1963, 404-427.

References

———. "Questioning the Place of Social Science Disciplines in Education." *Teachers College Record*, 69:1, 1967, 69-74.

———, and Donald W. Oliver. "Education and Community." *Harvard Educational Review*, 37:1, 1967, 61-106.

———, and Donald W. Oliver. *Clarifying Public Controversy: An Approach to Teaching Social Studies.* Boston: Little, Brown, 1970.

Nisbet, Robert A. Interviewed by Robert W. Glasgow in *Psychology Today*, December, 1973, 43-64.

O. M. Collective. *The Organizer's Manual.* New York: Bantam, 1971.

Oliver, Donald W., and Fred M. Newmann. *Public Issues Series,* 30 booklets. Columbus, Ohio: Xerox Education Publications, 1967-1973.

———, and James P. Shaver. *Teaching Public Issues in the High School.* Logan: Utah State University Press, 1974; first published by Houghton-Mifflin, 1966.

Oppenheimer, Martin, and George Lakey. *A Manual for Direct Action.* Chicago: Quadrangle, 1964.

Panel on Youth, President's Science Advisory Committee. *Youth: Transition to Adulthood.* Chicago: University of Chicago Press, 1974.

Payne, David A. (ed.). *Curriculum Evaluation: Commentaries on Purpose, Process, Product.* Lexington, Mass.: D. C. Heath, 1974.

Piaget, Jean (1937). *The Construction of Reality in the Child.* New York: Basic Books, 1954.

Ratcliffe, Robert H. (ed.). *Justice in America Series.* Boston: Houghton-Mifflin, 1970.

Raths, Louis E., Merrill Harmin, and Sidney B. Simon. *Values and Teaching: Working with Values in the Classroom.* Columbus, Ohio: Charles E. Merrill, 1966.

Rawls, John. *A Theory of Justice.* Cambridge, Mass.: Harvard University Press, 1971.

Rest, James, Elliot Turiel, and Lawrence Kohlberg. "Level of Moral Development as a Determinant of Preference and Comprehension of Moral Judgments Made by Others." *Journal of Personality*, 37:1, June 1969, 225-252.

Ridgeway, James. *The Politics of Ecology.* New York: Dutton, 1970.

Robinson, John P. *Public Information about World Affairs.* Ann Arbor, Mich.: Survey Research Center, 1967.

———, Jerrold G. Rusk, and Kendran B. Head. *Measurements of Political Attitudes.* Ann Arbor, Mich.: Survey Research Center Publication, 1968.

Rogers, Carl R. *Client-Centered Therapy: Its Current Practice, Implications, and Theory.* Boston: Houghton-Mifflin, 1951.

Rosen, Robert. "Do We Really Need Ends to Justify Means?" Center for the Study of Democratic Institutions, *Center Report*, February 1974, pp. 29-30.

Ross, Donald K. *A Public Citizen's Action Manual.* New York: Grossman, 1973.

Schein, Edgar H., and Warren Bennis. *Personal and Organizational Change through Group Methods.* New York: Wiley, 1965.

Schmuck, Richard A., and Patricia A. Schmuck. *Group Processes in the Classroom.* Dubuque, Iowa: Wm. C. Brown, 1971.

Schwartz, David C. *Political Alienation and Political Behavior.* Chicago: Aldine, 1973.

Scriven, Michael. *Primary Philosophy.* New York: McGraw-Hill, 1966.

Slater, Philip. *The Pursuit of Loneliness: American Culture at the Breaking Point.* Boston: Beacon, 1970.

Smith, M. Brewster. "Competence and Socialization," in John A. Clausen (ed.), *Socialization and Society.* Boston: Little, Brown, 1968, pp. 270-320.

Special Task Force to the Secretary of Health, Education and Welfare. *Work in America.* Cambridge, Mass.: M.I.T. Press, 1973.

Steinitz, Victoria A., Prudence King, Ellen R. Solomon, and Ellen D. Shapiro. "Ideological Development in Working-Class Youth." *Harvard Educational Review,* 43:3, August 1973, 333-361.

Thelen, Herbert A. *Dynamics of Groups at Work.* Chicago: University of Chicago Press, 1954.

Thorson, Thomas L. *The Logic of Democracy.* New York: Holt, Rinehart, Winston, 1962.

Tyler, Ralph W. *Basic Principles of Curriculum and Instruction.* Chicago: University of Chicago Press, 1949.

Veatch, Henry B. *Rational Man: A Modern Interpretation of Aristotelian Ethics.* Bloomington: Indiana University Press, 1962.

Verba, Sidney, and Norman H. Nie. *Participation in America: Political Democracy and Social Equality.* New York: Harper and Row, 1972.

Vlastos, Gregory. "Justice and Equality," in Richard B. Brandt (ed.), *Social Justice.* Englewood Cliffs, N.J.: Prentice-Hall, 1962, pp. 31-72.

Walberg, Herbert J. (ed.). *Evaluating Educational Performance: A Sourcebook of Methods, Instruments, and Examples.* Berkeley: McCutchan, 1974.

Warnock, G. J. *Contemporary Moral Philosophy.* London: Macmillan, 1967.

Wehlage, Gary G., Thomas S. Popkewitz, and H. Michael Hartoonian. "Social Inquiry, Schools, and State Assessment." *Social Education,* 37:8, December 1973, 766-771.

Where It's At: A Research Guide for Community Organizing. Boston: New England Free Press, 1970 (est.).

White, Alan R. (ed.). *The Philosophy of Action.* Oxford, Eng.: Oxford University Press, 1968.

White, Robert W. "Motivation Reconsidered: The Concept of Competence." *Psychological Review,* 66, 1959, 297-333.

―――. "Competence and the Psychosexual Stages of Development," in M. Jones (ed.), *Nebraska Symposium on Motivation.* Lincoln: University of Nebraska Press, 1960, pp. 97-141.

―――. "Ego and Reality in Psychoanalytic Theory." *Psychological Issues,* 3:3, 1963.

References

———. "The Concept of Healthy Personality: What Do We Really Mean?" *Counseling Psychologist*, 4:2, 1973, 3-12.

Wilson, John, Norman Williams, and Barry Sugarman. *Introduction to Moral Education.* Baltimore: Penguin, 1967.

Wisconsin Youth for Democratic Education. *A Student's Book.* Madison: Coalition for Educational Reform, 1972.

Worrill, Conrad. "Institution and Power: The Role of These Concepts in Secondary School Social Studies Curriculum Development." Unpublished dissertation, University of Wisconsin, Madison, 1973.

Index

academic freedom, 48, 64-65
action, 18, 19, 62, 97. *See also* social action
active-passive, 35
Adelson, J., 58
administration, 126-133. *See also* organization skills
adolescent development, 57-58. *See also* psychological development
adolescents, 68, 105-106, 119
advocacy skills, 78, 88-89, 116
alienation, 63(n). *See also* powerlessness
Alinsky, S., 89n, 103
Allen, H., 92n
Almond, G. A., 48, 49n, 65, 66
Apple, M., 151n, 153
Aries, P., 57
authority, 142-143
Baier, K., 29n
Bennis, W., 90n
Berelson, B., 51
Beyer, B. K., 84
Brand, M., 12n, 19n
Campbell, A., 48
career education, 25
causes, 95-96, 101-102, 143-146
Center for New Schools, 23n
Center for Youth Development and Research, 59n

Chapin, J. R., 84
Chesler, M., 67
citizen action curriculum: rationale for, 41-75; consequences of, 60-70; components of, 76-79; place in secondary curriculum, 111-121; development strategy for, 161-164
citizen participation, 45-46, 48-54, 55, 65-69
citizenship education, 3-6
Citizenship Education Project, 24
Coleman, J. S., 18n, 27, 36, 58n, 74, 84, 114
collective action (and cooperation), 86, 89-91, 106, 107, 108, 134-136
commitment, 93-95, 123
communication, 116. *See also* advocacy skills
community involvement, 6-11, 111, 125
community needs, 60-61
community relations, 129-131
community resistance, 59-70
community resources, 24-25, 56, 129-131
community teachers, 130-131(n)
competence, 12-40, 58, 122-123; defined, 12-13

competency-based models, 105-108
compromise, 99-100
conflict, 65-68
Conrad, D., 57
consent of the governed, 46-54, 68, 71-75
cooperation, *see* collective action
counselor, 117, 132, 149
Cox, C. B., 84
Cox, F. M., 89n
Crabtree, C., 84
critical thinking, 4-5, 23, 84-85
democratic process, 46. *See also* consent of the governed
Dewey, J., 19, 34, 37, 47
disciplines, 4, 5, 62, 84-85, 113
Dowtin, K., 106
dropouts, 51-52
effectance, 33-35, 52-53. *See also* competence
efficacy, *see* effectance
English, 112, 113, 116, 118, 119
environmental competence, 12-40, 75
equality, 47, 71, 81, 83. *See also* moral deliberation
Erikson, E. H., 36, 38n, 94, 100
evaluation, 22, 153-157, 160
facilities, 126
Fraenkel, J. R., 84
Frankena, W. K., 29n
Freire, P., 38, 99n
Fried, E., 35
Gardner, J. W., 92n
general education, 73, 75
Gillespie, J. A., 5n
Gottlieb, D., 101n
grading, 157-160
Greene, J. S., 92n
Gross, R. E., 84
group process, 78, 89-91, 116-117, 147-148
Hampden-Turner, C., 38n, 99n
Hampshire, S., 12n, 29n
Hanson, D. J., 127
Hare, R. M., 29n

Harmin, M., 31
Hartoonian, H. M., 107n
Holden, M., 89n
Huenefeld, J., 92n
Hunt, M. P., 84
identity, 36. *See also* Erikson, E. H.
implementation, 161-164
individualism, 37-38, 134-136
influence in public affairs, 4, 42-46, 76-79, 86-88
inquiry, 4-5, 23, 84-85
Institute for Political-Legal Education, 59n
instruction: organization of, 138-143
integrity, 99-100
intentions, 12-16
interpersonal relations, 90, 95-97, 99
Jencks, C., 20n
Jones, W. R., 92n
jurisprudential reasoning, 81-82, 88
Kahn, S., 92n
Kanter, R. M., 94
Kaplan, A., 84n
Kohlberg, L., 31(n), 32, 34, 47, 71, 80, 81(n), 82, 106, 118
Lakey, G., 92n
Lamm, Z., 132
Leming, J., 33n
liability, 127-129
life adjustment, 166
Lockwood, A., 31n, 80
Luft, J., 90n
Lurie, E., 92n
management, *see* organization skills
Marian, B., 85n
Marsh, D., 105
Maslow, A. H., 36, 38n
Massialas, B., 84
Matthews, D. R., 51
Mayer, R., 31n, 80, 106, 118
McKay, B., 92n
Merelman, R. M., 85n
Metcalf, L. E., 84
Michael, J. R., 85n
Milbrath, L. W., 48
Miles, M., 90n

Index

moral agent, 29, 30, 33, 37, 39
moral deliberation, 38, 44-45, 77, 79-83, 86(n), 112-114
moral education, 31-33
morality, 29-33
Mosteller, F., 20n
motives, 100-103, 122
Moynihan, D., 20n
Myrdal, G., 71
Nader, R., 92n
National Association of Secondary School Principals, 59n
National Commission on Resources for Youth, 59n
neutrality of schools, 45, 63-65, 151
Newmann, F. M., 24, 31, 46, 71, 74, 80, 81, 106, 132
Nie, N. H., 49(n), 50(n), 51, 53, 69n
Nisbet, R. A., 39n
objectives (educational): vs. activities, 8-11, 17
Oliver, D. W., 24, 31, 71, 74, 80, 81, 106
O'Neil, R., 58
openness, 93-95
Oppenheimer, M., 92n
organization skills, 78, 91-92, 117
Panel on Youth, 18n, 27, 58n
paternalism, 133-134
Patrick, J. J., 5n
Payne, D. A., 153
Piaget, J., 34, 81
pluralism, 64-65
policy goals, 79-86, 97
political-legal process, 4, 5, 78, 86-88, 115-116
Popkewitz, T. S., 107n
power, 86-88, 97-99. *See also* powerlessness
powerlessness, 1-3, 51-53, 123
practicum, 112, 119, 143-148
progressivism, 166
Prothro, J. W., 51
psycho-philosophic concerns, 78, 92-105, 117-118

psychological development, 33-38, 57-58, 81
public affairs, 41-42, 51-55, 65-70
Ratcliffe, R. H., 88n
Raths, L. E., 31
Rawls, J., 47, 53, 71
reflection, 18-20, 62. *See also* critical thinking
relativism, 71, 80
Rest, J., 81n
Ridgeway, J., 88n
Robinson, J. P., 48, 50, 65
Rogers, C. R., 38n
Rosen, R., 34n
Ross, D. K., 85n
Schein, E. H., 90n
Schmuck, P. A., 90n
Schmuck, R. A., 90n
school relations, 131-133
Schwartz, D. C., 49, 50, 63n
Scriven, M., 47
secondary curriculum: environmental competence in, 20-26; reforms in, 22-25; citizen action in, 111-121; instructional climate, 133-137
self: self-oriented competence, 15-17; actualization, 36; realization, 53; education, 101; assertion, 133-134
Shaver, J. P., 24, 80, 81
Simon, S. B., 31
skills, *see* advocacy skills, group process, moral deliberation, organization skills, political-legal process, social policy research
Slater, C., 106n
Slater, P., 39n
Smith, M. B., 12n, 35
social action, 6-11; defined, 8, 54-55; projects, 55, 59; roles, 97-99, 102-103
social issues, 24. *See also* public affairs
social philosophy, 70-72

social policy research, 77, 83-86, 114-115, 143
social reconstructionism, 166
social studies, 112, 113, 114, 115, 118, 119
socialization, 27-28, 39, 58n, 74
Steinitz, V. A., 106
stress, 66, 95, 104, 118, 149
student projects, 143-148
students: rights, 22-23; selection of, 121-126. *See also* adolescents
Sugarman, B., 29n
teacher preparation, 57, 148-150
teacher roles, 148-152
Thelen, H. A., 89n
Thorson, T. L., 47
Turiel, E., 81n

Tyler, R. W., 105
values, 5, 23, 32, 71, 79-83, 136-137
Veatch, H. B., 80
Verba, S., 48, 49(n), 50(n), 51, 53, 65, 66, 69n
Vlastos, G., 47
volunteer programs, 26, 143-144(n)
Walberg, H. J., 153
Warnock, G. J., 82n
Wehlage, G. G., 107n, 153
White, A. R., 12n, 19n
White, R. W., 12n, 17n, 33, 34, 35n
Williams, N., 29n
Wilson, J., 29n
Worrill, C., 106
youth: isolation from adults, 27-28. *See also* adolescents

DISCHARGED

JUN 07 1992